DEPLOYED

DEPLOYED

The Survival
Guide for
Families at War

STANLEY HALL, PhD

Published by Familius LLC, www.familius.com

Familius books are available at special discounts for bulk purchases for sales
promotions, family or corporate use. Special editions, including personalized covers,
excerpts of existing books, or books with corporate logos, can be created in large
quantities for special needs. For more information, contact
Premium Sales at 559-876-2170 or email specialmarkets@familius.com

Library of Congress Catalog-in-Publication Data

2013948924

pISBN 978-1-938301-67-4
eISBN 978-1-938301-75-9

Printed in the United States of America

Edited by Emily Smith
Cover Design by David Miles
Book design by Maggie Wickes

10 9 8 7 6 5 4 3 2 1

First Edition

Table of Contents

Introduction

This book can help serve as a training manual for our country's military families that have been thrown into the heat of the battle and are looking for answers and direction. The service members I talk to often share how they love their work and even the trainings and deployments, but they don't know how to handle their work and family relationships. This book is written based on my experience of what service members and their families need to hear so they can bring their relationships to a new level of excellence.

Thousands of people join the armed forces every year voluntarily. They consider it an honor to serve in our military. Their spouses, children, and families-of-origin in a way also join the military. Just as in World War II, when women and children supported the work effort through their labors, we can support our service members by learning more about the hazards—both physical and emotional—that try and afflict military families. The ways that families can be affected by military living are innumerable, and it would be impossible to try and outline each of them. You'll find that this book is written with guidance based on principles that can be applied to most situations. Not every principle that works is mentioned here, but this book is a good start. Other books that I would recommend to service members and their families are included in the appendix, along with phone numbers, Internet sites, and other resources I recommend. The Department of Defense has gone to great lengths in the last several decades to provide quality family services on each of its forts, bases, and auxiliaries.

I am a marriage and family therapist with over a decade of practice and have worked on the marine base in Twentynine Palms for the past four years. The principles that I learned while in school have universal application and have served me while working in an alcohol and drug treatment center, a church-based social services clinic, a community mental-health clinic, and on base in the navy hospital and the Marine Corps Family Advocacy

Program. I think of each new principle that I learn as a tool to put on my tool belt. Each piece of equipment that service members are given may have many applications that they learn about in training and apply maximally in combat. Think of these principles in the same way.

Joining, starting, or creating a family is like being thrown directly into combat with only what training your family-of-origin has offered you. One concept I love and emphasize is the irony of paradox. A paradox is anything that, against one's known logic, seems to act contrary to how it should. Relationships are full of paradoxes; they seem to define relationships. They are like the Chinese finger traps that only lock down harder as you pull away and loosen as you slowly push your fingers together. For example, parents who try to force their children to get ready faster often end up slowing the process down considerably. Service members who want to provide for their families or make their families proud by joining the armed force may sometimes find themselves with opposite results if they fail to process combat fatigue and prioritize needs.

Most marriages don't work and families fall apart. It isn't because the people aren't properly matched or have too different of personalities, as people like to say. It is because they don't have the skills and haven't aligned their desires. Don't worry about whether the person you married is your soul mate. If you are both willing to try, then make them your soul mate. To illustrate this point, I will often point to opposing walls in my office and ask clients to imagine a long line from one end of the room to the other. Then I ask them to imagine that a little more than half the distance of that line includes all the people who dated and then broke up for some reason. The remainder of the line is all the marriages that have ever been entered into, which is cut in half again with divorces. With now only a fourth of the line left, make your best guess at how many of those marriages include people that are satisfied with their relationships. How many of them can say that they would marry that person all over again and that they couldn't possibly think of leaving? The line gets a lot shorter. Some of my clients that I share this analogy with guess that about 90 percent of the remaining marriages are actually unhappy, some say half, and I'm not sure, but they are the minority of humans. Is it because they *just are* unusual people who were born to have happy marriages? Or is it because they are *doing* something unusual? I would like to believe that all of us can be in a happy relationship whether we are in the military or not. I would like to believe that the principles are the same. Sometimes being in the military is an advantage to a relationship, and sometimes it may be a disadvantage, but it certainly doesn't preclude anyone from the family of their dreams.

Parents, siblings, youth/children, and extended family members who are reading this book to better understand their active-duty family members will find that the same principles that make a happy marriage can be applied to making a happy family with kids and extended family. Don't ever give up on another human being; we all have value. The adult you see before you is in God's eyes as precious as a newborn child.

"The basic building block of good communications is the feeling that every human being is unique and of value." — Unknown author

This Isn't What I Signed Up For!

Serving one's country by joining the military is an honor that is unparalleled by any other line of work. More often than not, though, it seems that young men and women sign up for the military and then are shocked by what occurs in basic training or boot camp. Even service members who knew it would be hard are shocked by the regimen. Three square meals a day and eight hours of sleep doesn't seem like enough when you're tasked to the limit each day.

One female service member described how she loved the rigors of boot camp and enjoyed the challenges of pushing herself to the limit both emotionally and physically. However, in the months that followed, she found herself struggling with sitting at a desk, learning from PowerPoint lectures, and tediously completing more paperwork once she was out of class. The monotony of formation, paperwork, and trying to get along with fellow service members are some of the hardest parts for many service members.

"Hurry up and wait!" is a common phrase among service members who push through the paperwork and assigned tasks and then . . . wait. Compared to service members' grandparents' World War II stories, being in the military can seem like the opposite of what service members expected.

The sheer enormity of a federal organization often leaves service members feeling like small fish in a large ocean. Men who were the high school quarterback stars and hometown favorites are quickly disillusioned of their stardom when a complete stranger with a higher rank assigns them trash pickup and doesn't care who they dated in high school. This disillusionment is not so different from what happens to most people when they leave home for work or school, but in the military you can't change your mind about leaving home. Far from home and with few, if any, familiar faces, young service members must now decide how they want to cope with their choice to serve. Highly motivated service members may find that their enthusiasm will carry them a long way if they have a good commander who nurtures excitement. Support from home, friends, and a desirable job assignment (e.g., military occupational specialty, also known as MOS) can leave some members with no complaints at all, but those not lucky enough to have this combination may find themselves suffering from malaise (i.e., an underlying worry, discontent, and dissatisfaction) or worse. Sometimes these troubles are drowned in alcohol and other mood-altering activities, which only prolong the pain and compound the problems. A sign on the road leading into the marine base in Twentynine Palms reminds service members that a first offense misdemeanor DUI in California can cost upwards of thirteen thousand dollars by the time the offender gets through paying fines, attorneys, towing, and more. Paying for that on a PFC (Private First Class) salary could take years, especially if the service member is placed on restriction and his or her pay is cut in half or eliminated by command.

Military service has no comparison when it comes to enforcing discipline. Individuals who might still be living in their parents' basements and playing video games are instead out late and up early to train for combat. These souls will sometimes profess their undying devotion to the military for providing the stability they needed during a vulnerable time in their life. Promotions in the military have also given these individuals consider-able leadership experience, which is rarely found on a high school diploma. These

Transpose successful principles of leadership from work to home.

experiences can help them when they return to the civilian world and potentially make them excellent leaders in the home if they can transpose successful principles of leadership from work to home.

The hero inside of each military member, whether a reservist or active-duty member, needs a lift from his or her family when times are tough and not as he or she expected; even the toughest heroes rely on others. At the end of a twelve-hour day, the service member may return home and need lots of attention and love or time to reflect and be at peace without interruption for a few minutes. He or she may expect his or her spouse to cook dinner, clean the house, tend to the kids, work part-time or full-time, and be happy to have the service member back from long days of train-ing. When instead the service member walks in the home and is immediately handed the baby and told to pick up his or her boots and utes (uniform worn in the field) he or she dropped on the ground, tension can run high.

The spouse who signed up to marry the tough service member may now be asking the same questions: "Is this what I signed up for?" Months or years of deployment with only sporadic phone calls or letters while the service member is in a combat zone seems like a far-off problem when hormones are high and love is in the air. Moving to a faraway, exotic place is not always what you dreamed it would be, or it could turn out to be way better than you ever imagined! One friend shared with me how she and her husband drove into Twentynine Palms, California, from a more lush part of the country and checked into a hotel without being able to see the city in the dark. Awakening the next morning with bright hopes and an eagerness to start her new life, she instead literally barfed by the door when she saw only arid desert and stark brown mountains with scraggly bushes. Unfortunately, her story isn't unusual, and I have heard numerous versions of it in counseling. A two-hour movie just can't depict the absolute boredom and anxiety that is often a part of military service. The action is so often a small blip followed by days of doldrums in between and standing guard in the heat of the day or all night in freezing weather.

Combat is often a stress-inducing, anxiety-provoking nightmare that can lead to lifelong problems or disability caused by any number of physical or mental handicaps, like post-traumatic stress disorder (PTSD) and traumatic brain injury (TBI). One nearby explosion can be enough to send a service member pummeling into the hard edges of a building or vehicle or against the nonforgiving rocks of Afghanistan or Iraq. The Kevlar helmets may keep heads from cracking open, but they can't always prevent a concussion. Waking from the explosion, these service members may find themselves in a daze and seeing stars. They shake it off and go on with their mission, assuming that their injuries are not attention worthy compared to others who may have lost a limb or who are bleeding more severely. Any time there is unconsciousness, the injury is considered mild TBI, and coupled with PTSD, it can cause amnesia, imbalance, high irritability, thinking problems, nightmares, difficulty sleeping, and serious relationship problems. You definitely didn't sign up hoping for that! Nevertheless, you may have known it was a risk and were willing to sacrifice your comforts for the good of your country. For the rest of us, these life-changing events may be surprises that we are ill-prepared to handle. Guidance in the rest of this book will help you and your family to recognize and deal with some of these tougher issues.

As they say in the navy, "Welcome aboard!" and "Damn the torpedoes, full speed ahead!"

Married in the Military

When I ask service members, "What's harder: Being married or being deployed?" they invariably answer, "Being married!"

Marriage is the hardest thing most of us will ever do. Relationships in general are taxing and burdensome for even the best couples. Let's focus on marriage for now, and we'll discuss kids in the military later. Research numbers posted in 2004 suggested that one in five marriages failed within two years after a spouse was deployed into a war zone. Even when adjustments were made for the young age that many enlisted service members get married, in comparing enlisted active-duty soldiers to their civilian counterparts, it was found that soldiers still have a higher chance of divorce. During his first enlistment (usually a four- to five-year contract), a male service member is likely to be gone on deployment for at least one year, and with deployment workups and other long trainings that can last for weeks in the field, there may not be a lot of time to work on a marriage. The strain on military families climbed significantly in the first decade of the new millennium because of the Iraq and Afghanistan operations. I know many families who in the last decade have deployed three times during a five-year contract. I believe the first five years of a marriage (in some marriages) could be considered the honeymoon phase, but most of the service members I've spoken to never even had a honeymoon. Money was tight and time was short. Their decisions to get married only a week or two before boot camp or deploying are romantic and usually filled with passion but don't always include a lot of long-term planning. "He promised me a wedding reception where all our family could attend," is commonly heard among military wives. I wish I could say the reception usually does happen eventually, but it doesn't. I don't think it is because husbands didn't have the best intentions or because they don't want it to happen now; it probably doesn't happen for the same reasons that it didn't happen originally—time and money are still short.

With promises to love one another forever and to have a big to-do marriage later on, many military couples settle with a justice of the peace or a Las Vegas wedding (especially if you live in Twentynine Palms!). They may or may not have had family present at the wedding, and like many marines I met, they may still be teenagers. The single most predictive factor of divorce is how young the couple was at the age of marriage. Couples can make it through a lot, but getting through youth seems to be the biggest challenge. Enlisted service members and spouses complain to me that they never really got to enjoy their youth like their counterparts living it up at college. They fantasize about getting to snowboard, dance, and sleep in late while skipping college classes. Some marital partners complain that they were rushed into their marriages and that they would like to have had the opportunity to date a variety of people before settling down, but instead they married their high school sweethearts and traded hedonism for asceticism in their new military housing. Jacey Eckhart, the director of Military.com's Spouse and Family Programs, suggests that you "Marry young. In your twenties. Then grow up, dammit." I agree. She cites how more than half of military members are married by age twenty-five and that male military members marry at a much younger age than civilian counterparts—but having a deep relationship with one other person is one of the greatest predictors of life satisfaction.

If you got married in your thirties, forties, or later, you may have been married previously but got divorced and now have hopes for a new future. You may fare better in your marriage than younger couples, or you may be so set in your ways that you are having trouble adjusting to someone else in your life. Essentially, no matter what your age, you will have to make adjustments to living with another person and sharing the most mundane and intimate details of your life.

Marital Leadership

A successful military unit is founded on good leadership; a combat force will follow their leader into the heat of the smoke thinking only of their duty and combat brothers when leadership is good. Spouses will also follow their partners into life's thickest trials when the leadership is good, but they aren't just followers—they are fellow leaders! "I'm not his PFC, and he's not my sergeant!" many a good wife has lamented. "He acts like I'm his boot and that he can kick me around or tell me what to do." The husbands then look at me as though they can't figure out why their wives aren't obedient like their military subordinates. "You have to be coleaders," I explain. "Marriage

For couples in the military, it is difficult to always give marriage a lot of attention because of work demands, but you can make a commitment to give it all you have.

7

requires two leaders, but if two partners always agree then one of them is not necessary," I say, paraphrasing William Wrigley Jr. Overall, your roles are to foster independence in one another and create a safe, loving environment where creativity and growth can occur. Tom Peters summed it up: "Leaders don't create followers; they create more leaders."

Marriage is the highest expression of human love, in my opinion, and it requires the most effort of any human activity. Like any military unit, it needs not only leaders but lots of attention and commitment. For couples in the military, it is difficult to always give marriage a lot of attention because of work demands, but you can make a commitment to give it all you have. Dual military couples have some advantages in being able to appreciate one another's problems, but sometimes competition between one another can stir problems. Avoid any speech or thoughts that would make your partner feel as if you were better than them, served in a more important position, or deserved more attention.

Marriage Skills

If you feel like you have a terrible marriage—that you and your partner don't get along well or your personalities are too different or you aren't soul mates—I say that's typical. It is typical for marital partners to lack the necessary skills to make a marriage work. The only way that you can get those skills is to actually learn them with hard work, diligence, practice, study, and training. These skills are as real and as tangible as the combat skills you might learn and practice in a military field operation. More often than not, people already possess the necessary skills and are already using them with friends and in their field work, but they haven't figured out how to transpose them over to the marriage. These marital skills include the ability to listen and understand with empathy, to abandon selfishness and genuinely care about other people's needs, and to sacrifice your own wants and sometimes needs to create something better in the future. I often say that men aren't socialized for marriage. More often than not, it is the man struggling most with necessary marital skills. Women grow up talking to friends for hours every day, are required to complete many domestic chores, and often have experience with child care. Most men actually have few close friends they can talk to openly, especially about emotions and relationship issues. In my experience, most men can't recall *ever* having another person cry on their shoulders, having to comfort a child before having their own, or having to work through an argument that was hard to resolve. Instead, most men are socialized to keep their emotions totally covered, not talk about anything that suggests genuine vulnerability, and not engage in hours of discussion unless it is with women that they are trying to seduce.

> Listen patiently and carefully until you understand. Don't exploit your partner's weaknesses; protect them as you would in a combat zone.

Men's socialization is important, and it is great socialization for things like overcoming fears, starting adventures, keeping male friends, providing and earning a living, negotiating, and doing cool sports or hobbies that attract potential mates. However, that isn't enough for the current demands and pressures that society and the military put on marriages. It isn't enough to survive difficult deployments. Marital skills should not be considered feminine simply because women are often good at them. Plenty of men have mastered them, and many more have learned them well enough to see the benefits!

Therefore, men often need a lot of training and practice, but if they have the desire to change, there is a lot of help available. In the meantime, the wife may have to very patiently identify what she wants to focus on first and recognize that it will take years for her husband to internalize most of these skills.

Communicating in the Military Marriage

Communication in the military is essential. Every branch has entire schools just to teach people how to keep open communication. If the communication goes down in your relationship, you are likely to see problems quickly. By communicating accurately with your heart in the right place, you can prevent a lot of problems. However, almost every military couple that comes in to see me says that they have *only* communication problems. They *only* want help communicating better and learning communication techniques.

Communicating is not enough, though; each party has to know what to do with the communication and they have to have the right intent and a willingness to adapt. Sometimes communication lessons turn into drama coaching and making sure you say things the *right* way. The one with the least amount of communication skills or the most fear to stand up to the other may back down in the face of the therapist's coaching.

My assumption is that whatever you are saying, you are saying it on purpose. You may have been in a hypnotic or spell-like state at the time, but your brain and body said it, not some nebulous in space controlling you. Somewhere deep inside of you, or maybe more superficially, you meant to say what you said. It may have been misunderstood by accident, and that's pretty normal, but that doesn't usually cause marital problems. Now, when it's misunderstood on purpose in order to twist the other person up, then it does cause problems. Nevertheless, what we communicate is more often than not a view into our true desires. In the military, goals and missions are usually clearly established on some level. Marriages need similar goals that both partners agree on so their communications can be framed within those goals. Examples of such goals include buying a house, raising a certain number of children, reaching a certain level of promotion in the military, being active in a church, or making a spouse feel happy and understood.

In my perception, miscommunications generally happen for two broad reasons:

1. The signal isn't getting through because words are not spoken clearly, words are defined differently, or there is something distorting the words, like a past or present trauma.

2. Priorities are misaligned, causing a person to create arguments in an attempt to satisfy what he or she believes is most important.

In every relationship, there are times that the first reason is applicable and other times the second reason needs investigation. Let's look at the first reason. In this case, both people have good intentions, but things are getting obscured. Sometimes the military marriage radio isn't getting a clear signal, and partners need to patiently move around or carefully tune themselves for better reception. In such cases, improving communication may mean turning off the TV or phone and turning to face one another without distraction. Assuming that partners have set aside time to talk and communicate, the next step may be spelling out the message slowly and clearly to one another. Problems like this are prevented in the military and airports by using the phonetic alphabet (e.g., Alpha, Bravo, Charlie, etc.) and using stock phrases that are understood by both parties. In a marriage, sometimes the words are clear, but they are defined differently, and our true intentions are not conveyed. Intentionally picking out certain words and asking what they mean to your partner may be the difference between a screaming match and a chance to laugh over the vast difference between one another's definitions. Couples often won't remember what they were arguing about, but they will inevitably remember how they felt at the time of the argument and how much effort their partners put into trying to understand.

When couples go from dating to marriage, they sometimes forget that they still need to spend hours talking about their hopes and dreams. Finding time to do this when you have kids or a busy schedule may mean staying up a little later than usual, talking on long drives, taking breaks from work to visit with one another at lunch, writing notes, or sending the kids into another room so you can talk.

Metaphorically, in my relationships with others, it is my responsibility to adjust my radio to get the signal better. It is unwise to just assume that the other's radio broadcasting or receiving is always at fault. For instance, if a man doesn't understand his wife, he shouldn't assume that it is because she is a bad communicator or too emotional. Troubleshooting may turn up simple problems and quick solutions for why the communications are not going through clearly. A good troubleshooter always first rules out all the quick fixes before taking apart the hardware or returning the item as defective.

In a healthy relationship, both partners will work through their initial defensiveness and identify what is contributing to a misunderstanding. A person who has just returned from combat or a person who is dealing with severe trauma from his or her past may have difficulty hearing anyone clearly until they are able to process the background sounds of interrupting trauma static. Such static may be important broadcasts from deep within oneself that need to be tuned into and understood before any other outside message can be transmitted or received clearly.

Gary Chapman, in his book *The 5 Love Languages*, points out that sometimes communicating love means learning your partner's love language, which may be vastly different from your own. You may prefer gift giving, while your partner views it as wasteful. Sharing time together may mean the world to you, while service represents the greatest expression of love to your partner. Especially at the beginning of a marriage, it is important to ask questions about what certain things mean to your partner. The meaning behind the words is important and may help you communicate your truest intentions.

Of course, communication is not always with words, and sometimes our intentions are broadcast loud and clear with our actions or failures to act. The second reason I believe people have a communication problem is because their intentions are genuinely unhealthy for the relationship. They have inappropriately prioritized their needs over the needs of their relationships and their partners' needs. A service member who blows his bonus money on a new sports car that he bought without consulting his wife has communicated clearly that he believes his desires are more important than his wife's trust in him. He may try to argue that he bought it for her, or that it was supposed to bring them closer together, but more than likely he is obscuring his true intentions.

If a husband didn't really want to help plan a child's birthday party, he may forget to tell his wife that he had duty the night they were supposed to plan it. Military wives regularly came into a therapeutic session with the primary complaint that their active-duty husbands forget so many important things. Sometimes these men had traumatic brain injury and legitimately had memory loss, but usually after assessing these men's memories, I discovered that their memories were well intact and they could remember many important work- and sports-related statistics, dates, and numbers. These men had prioritized the things that were most important to them and had taken the time to remember them.

Unfortunately, when something is explained that clearly, it often causes people to go on the defensive and even get angry. He or she may sullenly try to point out his or her own partner's failings, thus going on the offensive. These communication attempts were clearly not made with the relationship's best intentions at heart. These individuals did not want their communication patterns spelled out so explicitly because it became plain that they had some changing to do. At home, the wife may have been fearful to explicitly spell out what she saw because of the anger or retaliation that would ensue. The husband's intentions in these cases may have been to simply buy what he wanted without having to answer to someone else, but what he actually communicated was "be silent, let me do what I want, and don't ask me to do things I don't want to do."

The man in such a situation may be oblivious to what he is actually saying, what intentions are driving his behavior, and how they are impacting the relationship. He may believe that he has the best intentions for the relationship and believe that his way is the right way. Maybe the reasoning is that if he is happy then everyone else will be happier too, so it's OK for him to pamper himself. Communication techniques, like standing on a tile and taking turns talking, can help a partner become more conscious of the impact of his or her behavior if implemented correctly, but the therapist has to be sensitive to the weaknesses and strengths of each partner and ensure that no partner is afraid of retaliation or holding back. If a partner were afraid of

> When couples go from dating to marriage, they sometimes forget that they still need to spend hours talking about their hopes and dreams.

the other partner, that therapist would actually be contributing to the dominant partner once again asserting his or her best wishes over his or her partner's. Everything can be twisted around if partners are not aware of their true intentions, especially if one partner assumes that whatever he or she does is with the relationship's best interest at heart.

In a war, it is OK to send out false messages and mess with the enemy's communication signals. Don't do that in your marriage; find ways to collaborate and remind yourself that on a team you have to make sacrifices. Men and women who are passionately in love find themselves frustrated that their partners have differing opinions. A military marriage should not be two armies battling one another so that one has to surrender their decision-making power to the other. If you truly believe your partner has a poor opinion of something, ask what good reason this wonderful person you married has for believing that way. Listen patiently and carefully until you understand. Don't exploit your partner's weaknesses; protect them as you would in a combat zone, because your own life may depend on your ability to protect them and strengthen them. In the marines, a saying is "Never leave a marine behind." No matter how poor your opinion of another service member is or how weak you perceive him or her to be, you don't leave him or her behind.

Sexual Frustrations

In a marital discussion, sex usually comes up. One marine shared his experience of how he and his wife were having sexual diffi-culties that required him to go very slow in approaching his wife. Successful sexual intercourse was dependent on how sensitive he was to his wife's emotions and how secure he made her feel. In the marines they say, "Slow is smooth and smooth is fast." When backing up a trailer, you paradoxically have to turn left to go right and right to turn left; it feels backwards, but it works. This marine learned patience early in his role as a husband. If he had tried to rush his wife, their marriage would have quickly slipped down-hill, and his impatience would have created new problems that would take even longer to process. As the folk saying goes, "Men are like microwaves, and women are like Crock-Pots." This met-aphor is probably true in more areas than just sexual foreplay. By the way, male service members who take time in the evening to help out with cleaning the home and cooking dinner and complete these tasks with good attitudes will help their wives have a little bit of energy left over for sexual activity after the kids go to bed.

Expectations

At the end of a long day, you may come home believing that your day has been terrible and hoping for a chance to unwind. Such a belief is not unjust, and you are probably deserving of such time. Working in the military is often strenuous, both physically and mentally. The physical labor may not even be nearly as taxing as the labor of getting along with your fellow service members. Upon arriving home, though, you find that your partner seems to equally feel that he or she deserves a break. One dual military couple related that they usually got in a fight whenever they got home. While discussing these fights, it became clear that the couple was actually competing in these fights to determine who had the worst day. The victor could take it easy and get a massage or lounge around the house, while the other would cook, clean, and pamper. The following day the cycle would repeat, and each person spent time trying to come up with the best arguments and the most convincing act to demonstrate his or her exhaustion to the other. This very act was exhausting. Just by naming the act, the couple was able to stop it and instead make a plan for what to do when they got home that allowed both to take rest breaks and still get home work done.

I told that couple that the first four minutes after you get home from work are the most important four minutes in the life of your marriage. These four minutes set the tone for the rest of the evening. During those four minutes, there should be no discussion of anything that could stir up drama. Don't mention all the bad things from the day, and don't talk about what tasks you're going to do that night or what you want the other person to do. Instead, just decompress together in those four minutes. Look into one another's eyes, cuddle, and as much as possible set a tone of patience and caring for the rest of the evening. When the four minutes are up and the timer goes off, you can jump up and go back to what you were doing with a more loving heart. Partners who implement this practice almost always find that they go back to what they were doing with more love in their hearts and a greater willingness to see the other person's point of view and help him or her.

I tell marines that when they get home, they better have done their rejuvenating in the car or at their place of work, because when they open the house door, they enter their second job. If you find that you are still struggling after the four minutes of peace when you get home, or your partner still isn't helping, or you are still emotionally distraught, take a few minutes to evaluate your expectations. Did you expect your new wife to be able to cook like your mother? Did you expect your new husband to be motivated (and able) to fix everything like your dad? These are skills that are learned over a lifetime, and rarely can newlyweds compete with old-timers in their sophistication of domestic talents.

When the couple mentioned above competed to win the other person's pampering with stories of exhaustion, they were failing to take responsibility for their own emotions. Each assumed that if he or she were the one who was most emotionally distraught, the partner should take over for him or her. First of all, that's fiction. You can't *make* another person feel good or bad. Yes, you can create a context that is conducive to them preferring to feel good or bad, but there have been plenty of exhausted soldiers overseas that chose to find joy curling up to sleep in the sand after a rough day of filling sandbags or worse. These individuals would normally not have been happy to sleep in such conditions, but sleep was a luxury at the time. Time and place utility say that we have a greater appreciation for the things we need but have little of at the time.

Unless you are in an abusive relationship in which your partner exploits your comforts and emotions, you should be able to find joy almost on demand with practice. It could require radical perspective changes, and you may have to go through a lot of sadness and grief first, but it is possible. A brief phone call while at work could seem like an annoyance, but when you're deployed, those moments of conversation can feel like the greatest pleasure. A bath is something I know marines miss when deployed. What if you could bring that gratitude for such a simple thing home with you? Take ownership of your own emotions; don't expect your partner to change your emotions. Learn to resolve your own emotions without having to stir up and see the same feeling in your partner. If your partner is always trying to make you deal with his or her emotions without considering yours, then express that observation. Sometimes you may need to assert the need to take a time-out and get away until you can resolve your own emotions and act normally.

Balance and Synergize

Everything requires balance. There is almost nothing in this book that couldn't be taken to some extreme in one direction or the other. When I encourage time-outs to resolve your emotions, you may start using them whenever you want to avoid a topic in your marriage. That would be extreme and wrong. If I encourage you to talk about tough topics, that doesn't mean that you restrain your partner from leaving until he or she stays and talks. If I say express your own needs, that doesn't mean *always* express your needs. Sometimes your needs will need to go on the back burner, like when your wife is having a baby, caring for a newborn, potty training a toddler, or coping with teenagers.

Men and women are different, but too often we focus on the differences and even see them as getting in the way of communication. Instead, we can see these differences as a way to synergize or make things better than ever. Stephen R. Covey highlights this in his book *The 7 Habits of Highly Effective Families*. This principle is similar to how good ideas often build on one another and even create whole new ideas with discussion.

When a problem arises in a marriage or family relationship, it can often be placed on a continuum with extremes on either end. One partner may talk too much, while another talks very little. Recognize the differences and appreciate that they exist between you and your spouse; in my experience, husbands and wives usually will grow to appreciate one another's views over the spectrum, even if they don't change their own opinions.

Traumas as Barriers to Communication

A couple came in to see me; similar to other couples I've seen, they were having communication problems and wanted me to help them. Each wanted techniques, I soon learned, for me to fix the other partner. I assessed for a while, and after several sessions I felt like we were making only mediocre progress. Then the husband said that their sex life wasn't good because his wife had been raped as a teenager. He wanted to know why she continued to brood over it and recall it, because he believed it was affecting their relationship. He had recently returned from a deployment, and I asked him if he had traumatic experiences while he was deployed. He detailed several scary episodes that he faced and how they continued to haunt his mind. He regularly saw the injured people even now, back in the United States, but only in his mind. He could be in a store, at home, or at work, and something would trigger his mind. Sometimes he even would start talking to the envisioned people and try to help them. While in combat, he had to suck it up because too many emotions messed with him, but now he found himself freezing up. I asked him if he liked that feeling and whether he thought he could control it. He admitted that it was involuntary and unwanted and that it left him feeling unsafe.

The smell of certain foods even made him nauseous because they reminded him of dying humans. His wife jumped in, saying that she had wondered why he wasn't eating and that she had tried to get him to talk, but he never would. In the end, they both admitted that they weren't talking to each other much about their past traumas because neither really felt safe. Both were having involuntary and unwanted symptoms. Respecting that each person was having his and her own internal conflicts and experiences helped this couple to respect why the other person was acting as he or she did. It wasn't that either one of them was crazy, as we often label one another when we don't understand motives. Instead, they needed help identifying that the other person was allowed to have conflicting experiences that were detracting from the relationship but needed processing in a safe environment. They were not intentionally trying to hurt one another but neither were they respecting the other person's individual and separate experience.

Wedding Invitations Story

John Gray wrote his book describing women as being from Venus and men from Mars—two separate cultures with two different languages. Little did Adam know as a single but engaged twenty-two-year-old marine how diverse the languages could be between the sexes. His story is similar to many a typical twenty-two-year-old male.

"Let's go look at wedding invitations together," Adam's wife said so innocently, almost giddily. About two months before Adam and his wife's wedding, he was following his beautiful bride to the section of the wedding store where several albums of wedding invitations sat on small wooden shelves. As she opened the albums, Adam stared in awe. What he thought would be a painless process of choosing between a dozen white cards turned out to be a wade through deep waters saturated with invitations so diverse that it seemed one had been created for every woman on earth who had ever even thought about getting married. Adam's breathing became a little more shallow, and he tried to hone in on only the ones that were very stereotypical invitations. This was a safe approach, so he could rule out more than half of the albums that were anything but white and quadrilateral. While his wife looked at one album, he pretended to look busy sorting through the other bland white cards that he knew people would look at, put on their fridges, and then throw away within a few weeks at best.

"What do you think about this one?" the sweet bride asked her loving groom, holding up a large white square card.

Pulling himself out of a self-righteous reverie, he peered down at a large white invitation with barely legible font. He actually liked the gold border, and it had a good presence. "It's great!" he said with a smile.

"Oh, well, what about compared to this one?" she said, holding up another large white invitation. No, it was a little off-white.

He crinkled his face a little. "What difference does it make? The first one's great!" he answered. *Didn't I just say that? Why are we still looking when we both liked the other one?*

She continued to stare at him with big, green, inquisitive eyes.

"Well, um, it looks a lot like the first one," he confessed with a shrug of his broad shoulders.

"Are you even looking at these?" she asked. She shook her head with contempt, staring back at the cards.

Adam continued to disinterestedly browse the album, but he tried to look busy by raising his eyebrows occasionally or shaking his head and pursing his lips.

He could sense his future bride's frustration and became a little nervous. He checked his watch; it had been twenty minutes, and he had to return to the fleet!

"But we still have several albums to go through," the bride said, pointing to the brown shelves.

"I know; you go ahead and look without me," he said. "Pick one out and I'm sure I'll love it."

The next evening, at her apartment, when Adam thought his part in the invitation selection was over and that he had successfully shared his opinion and would no longer be needed, she said, "I've been thinking about the invitations." She looked deep into his eyes.

What was she looking for? Oh, he hated this invitations business. Adam had hoped that by now she had gotten the message that he wasn't interested and that she would have moved on like a normal girl and finished the rest of this wedding planning with her girlfriends and sisters. Lucky for Adam, his fiancé wanted more for their marriage, and she was picking this battle on purpose.

"Did you pick one out?" Adam asked, smiling hopefully.

"No, I want us to pick one out together," she answered.

His face fell, the smile fading. "It would actually be fine with me if you and your girlfriends, or your sisters, or even your mother, selected one."

"I want you to help me," she answered.

He sighed deeply. "OK, I have a little time tomorrow. Let's go back and have a look."

The next day, he tried to focus his attention on the invitations. He was tired from staying out training until late in the night and was determined to get this done.

"I hate those ones," he announced with disgust, pointing at the entire album of eccentric-colored invitations.

"Are you sure?" she replied, studying the album.

Looking at her askance, he dared her to open the album again.

"You're right," she said filing the book back on the shelf.

This was taking forever. Again, he looked at his watch. It had only taken fifteen minutes again, but it had felt like an hour. Why did shopping take so long? Out loud, Adam announced triumphantly, "Well, at least we've narrowed it down to these two." They were the same two they had looked at the first day, which he had previously declared as "great."

"Why don't we keep thinking about it, and we'll make a decision later?"

"No, let's just pick now," Adam whined.

"No, I just can't decide," she said with frustration.

The proud marine hung his head in defeat.

Adam and his bride did get married, and they did finally choose the large white invitation with the gold border, and it was great, but Adam missed out on what could have been an amazing hunt with his wife. A contentious dispute that lasted for weeks could have potentially been ended in maybe an hour. What was missing? Care. Adam didn't care and wasn't interested. Sure, he had made a sacrifice to participate in the activity that he thought of as only a female activity, but his effort was patronizing at best. He wasn't willing to devote the energy his bride needed to connect on a deeper level with him. Many service members I talk to often like fishing, hunting, playing sports, and watching games. Even more, they like doing these things with people they love. Women often like shopping, scrapbooking, or just talking. Whatever your preference, you probably enjoy sharing it with another person. Let's talk fishing. Most fishers *care* more about the activity than the actual fish. If they really just wanted a fish, they would have bought it at the market. They *care* about who is there to witness the activity with them. Dads might take their sons fishing because it is an activity that helps them talk. Mothers might take their daughter's shopping because the shopping center is a place where they can connect. The setting is important, and each person's attitude and level of caring is even more important. Learn to appreciate the things that are different about your partner or family member. Try to understand why they like things and the meaning the things have for them. Appreciating the differences will allow you to synergize and produce more meaning and joy than ever.

Most fishers nowadays enjoy catch and release, and many a happy woman has returned from shopping with no purchases. The walking, the fresh air, and being with friends or others who enjoy the activity were what made it fun.

Perhaps you are like the wife I spoke to who pondered out loud why it was so hard to get her husband to participate in decision making with her. I thought of the invitation selection experience and then recalled having once viewed the changing of the guard at the Tomb of the Unknown Soldier in Arlington, Virginia. In this tomb that honors all the fallen service members that died in wars lie the remains of one unidentified soldier. There are specific lines and movements that have to be done just right for the exchange to be successful. The honorary changing of the guard isn't about changing the guard; it's about the process of ceremoniously honoring the sacrifices of others—the right way.

Maybe the reason couples aren't connecting in today's shopping and hunting experiences is because they aren't treating it enough like a ceremony. They aren't investing enough energy in the process that could lead to happy communication. The process could even be eating breakfast together, but there needs to be enthusiasm and an investment of energy in learning how to do the process in a way that facilitates closeness. I'm not talking about avoiding topics to prevent a fight, but neither am I talking about picking fights just to have something to talk about. My theory is that couples who often have nothing to talk about after being together for a while have closed too many doors on one another. They have made too many topics off-limits. Then, when one of them meets somebody new and finds that he or she can talk about these topics, he or she is happy again. Why not just revitalize the relationship with your first love by making those topics discussable again and swallowing the ego barriers?

The process of fishing or watching a game together can be compared to women's enthusiasm to shop or talk on the phone, because these women are being respectful of one another. Talking with other women while choosing certain items and dismissing others seems to be a ceremony that women have developed and mastered among themselves, made a part of their culture, and then passed on to the next generation. Unfortunately, most men have not been included in or refused to be a part of this inter-generational transmission of shopping etiquette and are generally clueless when it comes to shopping and choosing items in a group setting. But this may be a key to connecting with your partner, and you may not have to do it very often if you are good at it. It may be the doorway to reciprocation so that your wife will actually sit down and watch a race with you—for maybe an hour, anyway. Then you can teach her how to watch it with appreciation for the details in the context of the overall picture.

Adam's wife didn't want to shop with her girlfriends or sisters when selecting the invitations; she wanted to shop with Adam, specifically because she wanted the closeness and memories with him that would come from it. She told him in specific words, but he didn't get it. What he needed was a coach or someone to take him through the drills and tell him what to do. The more time a couple takes to coach one another on how to be in the process of living with the other and are willing to be coached, the closer they will become to one another. When you do this, you will be cultivating a vision together and learning a common language; that is the essence of communication.

Summary

Healthy marriages don't happen by chance, and they can't be left to whimsy and mood but neither can they be enforced. The military relies on good leaders, and your marriage demands that you both take the lead in making good things happen in your relationship. You have a lot of responsibilities, and success is dependent on how accountable you make yourself to the demands that are placed on you. Marriages aren't always a joy ride filled with pleasurable memories, but neither should they always be descents into hell. Communication in a marriage is difficult and often requires that you pay close attention to the process of what is occurring between the two of you and then sensitively make adjustments so you can tune in to one another. By investing time and energy into your marriage, you will find that you are creating memories and traditions that will motivate and inspire you during the tough times down the road when a leader is most needed in the home.

A Few Principles of Happy Families

If you could have a miracle tonight, what would it be? More money? When I ask this question, most people actually say they want happiness and better relationships. Military families who can agree that their primary goal is to be happy together have a goal in sight, a common vision that they can pursue and align themselves with. Having a common vision is a principle of success.

A principle is something that is, according to its definition, unchanging; it may be subject to higher principles, and their applications may vary depending on the context, but they are unchanging. A principle can guide a couple from wherever they may be in the world, similar to how a star constellation might guide a boat through markerless oceans. Families who neglect to learn how to navigate by these constellations are leaving their relationships to chance. In Afghanistan and Iraq's more remote areas, street signs and clear maps are hard to come by, and denizens might direct you based on animals tied to trees or fruit trees that you might pass along the dirt roads. As helpful as these persons are trying to be, their directions are not always clear or identifiable. Most folks prefer an accurate map with street names and street addresses that are unlikely to change. That's what I'm offering in this book: a map with directions.

Take a minute to think of what principles you have already been applying in your life. Last time you spoke to your commander (boss), what principles kept you from yelling at him or her? While driving in traffic, don't principles keep you from driving on the wrong side of the road, swerving off the road to pass cars, or zipping through red lights? Principles keep you safe and help you get along with other people. Ultimately, every good leader hopes that his or her troops will learn correct principles and apply them to their unique responsibilities. This alleviates the burdens of the leaders and gives them confidence to let their troops act responsibly and in good faith.

Paradoxes of Patience

One question I regularly ask service members is whether they have one leader in their command that they like talking to when they have a problem. Inevitably, they describe a patient leader that listens to them. Then they compare this patient leader to a less impressive leader who doesn't want to hear their thoughts or context and ends up making a lot of mistakes. Perhaps it is our lack of patience in the first place that causes us to overlook this prerequisite principle. Patience is an indicator of selflessness and a true principle; the double yellow is an essential road marker similar to how the principle of patience is an essential guide for families. When we are patient with our family members, we demonstrate unwavering love and sacrifice; we are expressing our faith in other people and our hopes that they will make good decisions and be faithful in return. As I mentioned in the first chapter, the military often requires people to hurry up and wait, but between family members, a better phrase is, "We'll wait on one another, no matter how long it takes." You aren't perfect, and you know sometimes family members need to wait on you or be patient with your weaknesses. Do you allow the same grace to them?

All friends and family members agree that the principle of patience is an absolute necessity while on deployment or waiting for a family member to return from deployment. And military kids agree that deployments take forever! As a child, it can be hard to adjust, and perhaps you are tired of people telling you that it will all be over soon. Finding a mentor, like a teacher, neighbor, sibling, or friend who has been through the waiting game can help you reframe your thoughts and find positive ways to view the distance that is created by deployments. If

> Adjust slowly. Don't try to fit in quickly and make everyone happy all at once.

you can, use the time to learn new responsibilities and help your caregiver/parent do work around the house. When your loved one does return home, he or she will be impressed how much you learned and how much you helped keep the family together.

Patience may be as important when your deployed loved one returns home because you have to adjust back to family life. Trainings, long hours at work, and weeks of being in the field can leave you lonely and impatiently waiting to return home. If you are a returning service member, I would suggest that you adjust slowly; don't try to fit in quickly and make everyone happy all at once. A gentle and patient approach will help you identify what things have changed since you left and build on them.

Focus on the present. Do not count the days; that seems to only slow things down. Instead, try to enjoy each day and every minute. Pack the days with fun and memorable experiences. Treasure the time to learn new skills and appreciate the new people you meet everywhere you go. Get to know someone you wouldn't normally talk to. Explore new philosophies and get to know the new culture that you may have moved into. Share your time (which you seem to have so much of) with others who might also need a listening ear. Take care of your own needs and find a peaceful center in yourself that remains strong while things change.

Transitions seem to always be occurring in our lives. Identify each new life transition as something that needs extra time to process. Go slowly over the metaphorical speed bumps, through the flashing yellow lights, and around the construction in your life. Sometimes it is helpful to think of transitions as a time to hit pause on everything else and focus on what is occurring. When a family member deploys, you put everything on hold to say goodbye; that is an example of transitioning patiently and putting your family first.

The smallest child can miss a parent. They often are the best examples of being patient when they play, loving the people around them, and appreciating small things that make life great. Service members who take the time to be with their kids every day after work will help children develop a secure attachment, this will help them survive deployments and long trainings.

The principle of patience can go a long way toward preventing physical and emotional injuries. In training, a service member understands that putting forth his or her best effort to learn how to do a dangerous practice perfectly will in the long run save more time than if he or she jumped in without training and got injured. An injury will take much longer to heal than waiting patiently to get it right. In family relationships, we often have to practice our relationship skills and allow for understanding to unfold in ourselves and in our family members. Most skills for being a successful family member are not really intuitive and don't occur naturally; they become manifest only after diligent effort and serious seeking. Even once you understand a skill or principle, you have to patiently teach it to the rest of the family.

Patience is something you do when you're on a military squad or sports team, and you patiently wait for others to complete their parts of the mission or make the plays. You've spent months or years studying and practicing the tactical movements, and now's your chance to put it in action. You wouldn't dare rush out into the middle of a combat zone by yourself and try to save everything. You carefully implement each practiced principle of combat as it seems to fit the context. If you had losses and you weren't as successful as you hoped you would be, you go back to practicing, evaluating, and making revisions to the implementation of the skills that you know work. Perhaps they were ill applied and would have fit better in a different context. In a family, it is important to accept full responsibility for your own actions and any shortcomings or weaknesses that you may have. Acknowledging them and slowly working on them can make you a better family member and help you appreciate others' weaknesses and your family member's efforts to strengthen them.

You may be impatient when there is an opportunity to move ahead (e.g., driving or career). You may be impatient whenever you can get away with it. As long as the risks don't outweigh the potential for gain, who cares if another person gets his or her feelings hurt? In my view, service members exemplify patience when they sacrifice years of their lives on deployment. Family members show the same patience in waiting during deployments. Patience is also shown in carefully considering family members' abilities and needs and prioritizing them ahead of your own needs, which are sometimes met last. Such patience is characteristic of a true leadership.

"Patience is faith in action," according to Stephen R. Covey in his book *The 7 Habits of Highly Effective Families*. It requires pursuing goals through waiting. Active waiting includes observing, watching, nurturing, and believing that good things will follow or that the person you are waiting on will find a way to fulfil their mission. Generally, there is much that can be done in terms of preparing and fortifying while waiting. One sergeant described to me how he spent his time waiting overseas by filling sandbags. This monotonous task was time-consuming, but after days of working, the soldiers created a sandbag structure that provided some relief from the desert exposure. The work kept them strong and gave them a way to direct their energy. When they returned from deployment, their spirits were high because they had been proactive and energetic with their time.

Humility Is Power

Whenever there is a hierarchy of power, such as is found in the military, and the potential to progress up a career ladder, you will find drama and discord as people try to impatiently jump ahead. There should be no individual ladder to climb in a healthy home; paradoxically, humbling yourself is sometimes the only way to get real respect and power. One service member clarified it all for me when he said, "Humility is power. It is what you get from being kept on the bottom. It is your reward for enduring adversity. Humility lets you keep your power. They can't take your humility away. It is what makes you wise. It is what helps you identify and compensate for weaknesses. If you are missing humility, people will always be trying to overthrow you." This insightful observation by this humble service member sums up servant leadership—the idea of working or serving as a leader rather than being catered to as a leader. Humility makes you somewhat vulnerable, but it is also the glue that bonds you to others and allows them to approach you with concerns and real solutions. Children exemplify this when they ask for help.

> Humbling yourself is sometimes the only way to get real respect.

In your home, you are already a leader by default, whether you are a parent or child. Recognizing your weaknesses will not cause you to lose power. At worst, it will open up a discussion between family members on how to help. Maybe consciously or unconsciously you think the secret to success really is to get ahead of others. After all, it may seem like only the impatient, selfish, and prideful people get promoted. If so, consider what happens when you apply this belief in your home. Adults will find themselves in constant contention with one another. Rather than sharing their resources, energy, and ideas, they will reserve them only to promote their own ideas. All family members involved will resent one another. A humble family member acknowledges others' independence and weaknesses without exploiting them. Military teams and units require that each member act independently while relying on others to also act independently, thus making them interdependent on one another to fulfill a mission. A glory seeker may get a lot of attention or even be able to steal honor from others, but in the end, he or she may be hindering the progress of even himself or herself when he or she is insensitive to the overall mission, because if the team loses, then he or she loses with them.

Humbling yourself means regularly relying on the strength of others to compensate for your acknowledged weaknesses, then giving them appropriate credit for their work. One service member in derision denied believing that a dependent wife's job was nearly as hard as his own. He ridiculed her needs and pleas for help at home. Yet, at the same time, he acknowledged her strength when he implied that she needed to do more to support him in his work. Unfortunately, he was missing out on an opportunity to humbly acknowledge his wife's work and strengthen her so that she could later strengthen him. Use your strengths not to embarrass others but to appropriately compensate, teach, and uplift. Acting in humility is assessing the military field operation later on to find out what errors were made and what strengths could have been used in compensation. Growth occurs when you learn from mistakes rather than ignoring them.

One of the biggest complaints I get from junior enlisted marines is that their knowledge and solutions are rarely heard or considered, yet they often have the most insight into how to do something more efficiently because they perform the same task all day. Is everyone in your family being surveyed for their insights and ideas? In your family, no one can be exempt from the principle of humility. Everyone either all wins together or all loses together, and losing even one family member to pride can be catastrophic to the family's later performance.

Taking Responsibility Versus Blaming

The highest functioning families are able to avoid blaming one another and focus on taking responsibility. When results are not forthcoming, they are able to identify mistakes that were made and make changes. Changes are focused on finding out how to prevent the mistake from occurring again. Families can't fire one another for mistakes; they can only build on their mistakes and responsibly identify their roles in a future solution. Parents are responsible for teaching children and children are responsible for chores, school, and acting respectably. These responsible actions are contrary to blaming another family member and identifying them as the primary problem. Small mistakes can be the stepping stones to greatness if proper tutoring and learning follows. It is OK to be sad after a mistake is made by yourself or another. It is not OK to yell, berate, and guilt-trip the other person to the point that they want to give up. Motivation to get better will include uplifting words and responsible language.

In the military, a service member making mistakes in combat training would not be eliminated simply for making a few mistakes. Patient leaders will help him or her identify what he or she is doing wrong and what needs to happen and then follow up to be sure it is done correctly. In the home, you are the leader. Even children have the opportunity to show leadership and responsibility in the home when they identify problems and make things right. In a home, you have responsibilities that only you can fulfill. Older siblings can show leadership and responsibility when they help younger children and avoid blaming themselves or others.

As a parent, it is easy to see how if a child breaks a vase in the home, it doesn't make you any happier if he or she lies on the ground and cries and bawls about his or her poor choice That would be blaming oneself. It will, however, make you happier if your child confesses, cleans it up, tells you that he or she isn't going to play baseball in the living room anymore, and comes up with a plan to pay for the broken vase with his or her allowance. That would be taking responsibility. In a way, all family interaction is a training experience, an opportunity to grow and recognize where change can occur, and an opportunity to make improvements and see each mistake as a learning opportunity.

I have counseled dozens of women who tell me that they are sick of hearing, "I'm sorry." They hate hearing it, because it doesn't mean anything. Examples include the husband chewing tobacco and swearing he has quit, then trying to hide receipts of purchasing it; maybe the husband was looking at pornography secretly and denies looking at it, even when the wife finds a browser history of it. When the wife finally corners him, he says, "Yes, I messed up. It is all my fault. I'm sorry." To the wife, that isn't enough if he does it again next week and again tries to cover it up. "What are you going to do about it?" the wife asks in frustration. Instead, the responsible husband needs to spend considerable time understanding what contributed to the problem and discuss plans for how he will prevent future mess-ups and be completely honest about potential future mistakes. Years of penitence and allowing oneself to be under some level of surveillance may be a way of taking responsibility.

If a teenager confessed to stealing cash but then continued to steal more in the future, would a confession be enough to show responsibility? No. Responsible parents would want the teenager to pay back the cash and talk it out. Parents will recognize their own responsibilites when they hide the cash better in the future and create consequences and punishments. Unfortunately, sometimes the teenager (like some adults) may actually get angry at the one who caught them stealing and believe he or she is above punishment. A responsible response includes frequent follow-up discussions, plan making, and open conversation about what happened and how it can be prevented. A blaming response turns into finger pointing, belittling, silence, and often anger from both sides with little resolution.

In the military, you are absolutely responsible for your every action and for any piece of gear that comes up missing. In a family, holding yourself to this same standard of excellence even if you could get away with it will ultimately make you much more trustworthy in future contexts. It is the only way to gain back trust, heal the emotional wounds, and pave a new path for healing.

Respect

All of us want respect, but it often becomes disproportionately important when it trumps other people's psychic boundaries or ability to act in self-defense from a physical or emotional attack. Respect is a principle that should be universally applied in all relationships. However, many former inner-city residents share with me how they aren't willing to give respect until they first get it. That makes no sense to me. If you are going to be in a working relationship, then respect needs to be mutually expressed, and who shares it first is irrelevant. Even if you don't trust someone, you still need to show respect.

Should I capitalize on my wife's weaknesses and exploit my wife's deficiencies? In combat, you would only do this to your enemies, but in the home we often do it to the one who should be our best friend. When we return home after the marital fight and find our partner still broken and crying, we can't understand why they haven't gotten over it already. We ask ourselves, "Don't they know that my needs come first?" Unfortunately, this entitled mindset can sometimes be more prevalent in those who are fighting a global war; some soldiers believe that they should be honored through indulgence. They may propagate the impression that others should forever be beholden to them. They may believe that the time they spent training, sacrificing in combat, traumatized, hurt, and grieving the death of friends merits them more

36

worthy of having their needs met first. More than one service member has openly shared this attitude with me and asserted, "I did this for you. Now you do something for me."

Fortunately, this is not usually the case, and most service members are not looking for recognition or entitlement. To some, though, this quid pro quo thinking sounds reasonable and fair, but it isn't. This same scenario plays out in the civilian world too, but in this scenario the attitude is, "I put in all these hours and gave you all this stuff, so you owe me." But what about the wife who didn't finish college or gave up a high paying job so she could move to a remote area? What about the partner who loyally stayed home alone for months, worrying that any day the phone or doorbell could ring with news of your death? These people are also suffering and sacrificing for their country and family.

Many mothers have expressed that they feel like single moms because their husbands are gone so often. Sometimes these mothers will even say that it is easier when their husbands are gone, because they don't have to worry about having dinner ready right on time, cleaning the house to perfection, and making sure the kids are perfectly behaved. Theirs is the responsibility alone at times to balance the bills and deal with schoolteachers and homework, youth sport practices and coaches, shopping, house and lawn care, kids' emotional problems, cooking, and social life while trying to be as supportive as possible for their active-duty family member. These partners want some recognition too and are hoping that their heroes will return home and treat them respectfully and equitably. When you get home from a hard day's work of serving your country, get ready, because the work has just begun at home!

Children are often the victims and perpetrators of disrespect. Parents are responsible for acting respectably to their children regardless of their children's actions. There is never an excuse for hurting a child, and more often than not children learn how to show respect appropriately by watching their parents. Practice using the same respect you showed your drill sergeant or that you currently show your commanding officer when interacting with your family. Senior officers and newly enlisted service members are all expected to show respect, no matter who they are interacting with in the military. Ideally in a family, each person will treat the other with utmost respect, even more so than if they were acknowledging a high-ranking officer. If each family member reciprocates and acts with unfeigned respect, each can negotiate, synergize, and expand his or her campaign.

Empathy and Emotional Intelligence

Respecting one another may not mean saluting one another at the doorway but simply being empathetic to one another's thoughts, feelings, and needs. The principle of empathy can help facilitate patience, humility, responsibility, and respect. Recently, two separate male service members asked me what empathy was; their wives kept saying they needed to learn it, and now I was telling them they needed it. We turned to the dictionary to get the most accurate reading. Empathy is "the action of understanding, being aware of, being sensitive to, and vicariously experiencing the feelings, thoughts, and experiences of another."

> Respecting one another may not mean saluting one another at the doorway but simply being empathetic to one another's thoughts, feelings, and needs.

Understanding, awareness, and sensitivity to *what*? To the feelings, thoughts, and experiences of others. This is a very difficult thing to do when one is not even aware of his or her own thoughts and feelings. A psychologist friend of mine, while working in the Deployment Health Clinical Center, found that even when she used her neurofeedback machine to create feelings of happiness in sailors and marines, they often did not have a name for what they were experiencing. She would patiently explain to them that they were experiencing joy, but it was as if they had never experienced it before and had no name for it. Her job, in this case, was teaching them emotional literacy. Women generally grow up in a sociological context in which emotional discussion is encouraged, but men can rarely remember the last time a male friend cried on their shoulder, if ever.

Unless your parents taught you about identifying and dealing with emotions and healthy relationships, you probably never learned emotionally intelligent ways to interact with others. If you are a parent, you can start now to learn about and model emotional intelligence for your children. If you are a child, you may want to proactively begin learning all you can about the life-changing benefits of becoming more emotionally intelligent. The unofficial approach in the military has historically often included directly or indirectly teaching service members to harden or deaden their emotions so they could operate in highly emotional contexts. There isn't time to grieve when a friend dies in the heat of combat, and a psychologically frozen soldier is a dead soldier. This approach may be the fastest way to get through a combat situation, but in the long run it may be the slowest, because it may prevent you from being able to ever return to combat. There is another way to deal with highly emotional contexts. More and more research is suggesting that the most emotionally intelligent individuals are the most capable of thinking in times of stress, and they are less likely to freeze. I am suggesting that empathy is one of those skills that emotionally intelligent persons possess and that it is associated with perceived relationship quality.

Combat is not the same as being in a family relationship, but I am using it as an example of how emotions are powerful things that can make life a lot harder or a lot easier, depending on how you deal with them. Someone who can't identify his or her own emotions or empathize with others may have a much more difficult time getting over problems that are combat or relationship oriented. In the heat of combat, service members do not have time to grieve, but when they return home and those emotional injuries are begging for attention, can soldiers sleep and return to normal functioning? If not, it will affect their family lives.

Sometimes the biggest, tallest, and toughest-looking men freeze when the gunfire starts in a real kill zone, whereas scrawny counterparts may function flawlessly, dragging the big guy to safety. Being fearless should not include being emotionless. A safer approach is being able to identify emotions and process them quickly to make coherent decisions that can save lives. Athletes and service members train daily to gain muscle strength and skills of awareness; you can make similar gains in emotional awareness and emotional strength by learning how to tune into your body's emotional language. The heart may not have a mouth to speak, but it does communicate with sensations. Choosing to ignore them is choosing to ignore important smoke signals from deep in your soul. When you are able to identify your own emotions and face your own fearful thoughts, you will be better equipped and emotionally available to help your family with their needs. To learn more about emotional intelligence, I recommend the book *Emotional Intelligence* (See Appendix C).

Summary

As parents, in-laws, children, and marital partners in the military, you have the opportunity to learn and practice many new principles of success in your family within the context of a challenging military context that may include weeks or years of separation. The rewards for diligently and patiently learning and applying effective principles can be incredibly satisfying. I think that is why so many join the military and start families every year—they know that the potential for increased joy is more likely in a family than when single. Patiently growing together as a family is a prerequisite to almost every other principle of growth in a family because everything takes so long to implement. Deployments are long separations that tax families to the extreme and require extreme patience. Family members who seek out ways they can be responsible and improve their interactions with others will benefit themselves as well as those they serve. As a service member, you are used to showing respect at work. Bring these skills home with you and use them in your interactions with others, modeling for your children, spouse, and in-laws the pride of military respect and discipline. Implementing and learning new skills requires humility, but this trait will make you a better leader and help you accept difficult circumstances. Humility will also elicit the respect of your family and help them feel safe expressing their fears, concerns, and feedback for you. Acquiring emotional intelligence will make you a more effective service member and person in general. The challenges of being in a family are enormous. Listening to the emotional concerns of each family member and appreciating how they may be different from your own can go a long way toward increasing mutual respect, love, and resilience. Creating these reserves and learning these skills will help you navigate and survive even the roughest deployment.

Growing Up with Sgt. Dad and Lt. Mom

Growing up with parents in the armed forces can be an exhilarating experience that includes touring military duty stations, climbing on tanks, watching helicopters and jets fly overhead, feeling the earth shake when bombs are dropped nearby in trainings, and getting to see your parent(s) in uniform. Moving between bases provides an opportunity to meet new friends and see new places. If you live on base, you may feel a sense of security knowing that your neighbors are fighting alongside your mom and/or dad.

There are many resources available to you on your base. Start with the youth programs and talk with a leader about how to get more involved and more knowledgeable as a child of active-duty parents. If you have more serious concerns, talk to the family services department on your base. You deserve to feel safe in your own home and neighborhood, and growing up doesn't have to include being bullied or belittled by peers or family members.

As a youth, you may feel inclined to join organizations like Young Marines, Junior Army ROTC, Air Force Space Camp, or other youth programs that your base may offer. The leaders of these organizations will help you learn more about what it means to join the armed forces and the discipline required for excellence. Most military bases have libraries with books written for kids just like you who have military parents (see http://www.booksformilitarychildren.info/). These books range from board books to young adult books. Reading these books can help you take pride in your parents' work and in your own experiences living on or near a duty station. Avoid hanging out with other teens or youth if they only have negative things to say about the military. Refrain from being negative yourself. There will always be things that could be criticized, but you will find much more joy as you take pride in your parent's work and enjoy the many perks available only to Department of Defense kids. Overall, being a child in a military family should be a positive experience. Your deployed parent may not be able to communicate with you because of technology or the type of mission that they are on, but you will find that writing them a weekly letter will give you a chance to express your own thoughts, fears, hopes, and emotions to them. On a daily basis, you should look for the positive things in your life and appreciate the reasons your parent(s) may have signed up for the military, despite any hardships it places on you or them. Sacrifice has always been a defining characteristic of the armed forces, and as a child you literally did not sign up for this life. However, you can make it a source of pride in your life by learning about the history of the branch of service you are a part of and learning about the list of heroes in that service. Be proud that your parent(s) can now be included on that long list of heroes.

Stressors That Parents Can Help Alleviate

As a parent, you are probably aware that children are under significant stress in our society in general. In the military, stressors are sometimes more easily identified, like moving, deployment, or having a parent killed or wounded in combat. The effects on children range from suicidal thoughts to hostile and violent behavior to extreme depression and school problems. It is critical that you as a parent are as knowledgeable and sensitive to your child's emotions and needs as possible. Find out what you can do to create the healthiest life possible for the kids that heroize you. Once again, the principle of responsibility comes into play because ultimately you as the parent are responsible for your child's well-being, not the government, teachers, coaches, or scout masters.

Such experts in their fields are helpful and should be utilized to the fullest. Sometimes counseling is necessary. Risë VanFleet, an expert in child therapy, proposes that Filial therapy helps parents find ways to connect with their children to alleviate the many challenges unique to military families. She explains:

> Military families face unique stresses with frequent moves and separations during deployments. Deployments and reunions necessitate substantial role changes. During times of war or heightened military alert, families encounter greater worry about their deployed relatives, especially when communications are prohibited or erratic. Injuries and sometimes death are difficult for everyone to think about or cope with. Children are vulnerable under these conditions and may display their anxieties through internalizing, externalizing, and trauma reactions. Filial therapy has been used with military families when they are intact and when they are separated by deployments. It helps strengthen family relationships, gives children an outlet for their concerns, provides parents with the tools needed to meet their children's emotional needs more fully, and offers parents substantial support during difficult times. Filial therapy can also help families develop or maintain the flexibility needed for constantly changing conditions.

Filial therapy teaches parents how to conduct Child-Centered Play therapy in their own homes and can help parents develop the relationship of love, warmth, and empathy that a family therapist would normally use to reduce problem behaviors in children. Developing and keeping these characteristics at home is hard work. The remainder of this chapter will hopefully clarify some important aspects and difficulties of the lives of military children. Keeping these points in mind will help in maintaining the positive emotions that your child needs to feel from you.

Moving and School Transitions

If you grew up in a military family yourself, you know that moving is always stressful, even if you do have someone else moving your belongings. Children will and should become attached to wherever you are currently living. You may not love the area and consider it only temporary, but to children whose frontal cortexes of the brain are not developed, the word *temporary* does not have any applicable meaning for resolving their attachment to the area. Everything is permanent to a small child. Even if a child has moved around several times already, and even if there were things he or she didn't like about the old place, and even if there are more family and friends in the new area, he or she will have difficulty adjusting. You may have grown up in a city or state that you consider your hometown, but military children who have lived all over the country rarely have the same affinity for this "hometown" and have trouble identifying it as part of their heritage unless it is where they have actually lived themselves. Your children are growing up on bases, forts, and stations where

> Nurture your children in their experiences and make them proud of who they are as children in a military family.

the culture and traditions of the military are picked up on whether you know it or not. The military culture that your children are adopting is not indigenous to just one part of the world but can be found wherever military families reside. Nurture your children in their experiences, and make them proud of who they are as children in a military family.

Studies evaluating military adolescents' transitions to new schools found that teenagers often had a reluctance to get close to friends and that peers sometimes were reluctant to get close them because they knew the military student would be moving soon. Extracurricular activities, which is how students often make friends, are often difficult for military children to get involved in because they are the new students and do not have a history with their peers. However, children and adolescents find their greatest connections at new schools through peers, and even one close friend can help a new military student adjust. Military youth who do the best in school have close associations with their parents, neighbors, and peers. A high level of support and care from mothers may in many instances be enough to prevent more significant emotional issues and conduct problems at home and school

Helping Children Cope with Sadness

Losing friends at school feels devastating to youth, but losing a parent to death or serious injury feels catastrophic. As a parent, your ability to maintain sanity and keep yourself together will make the biggest difference in how your children cope with loss. Seek out whatever outside help you possibly can in terms of professional service to make you more available for your children. Children should have an opportunity and forum to discuss their own feelings of loss and sadness. They should be encouraged to implement their own creative outlets through play and, if they are old enough, talking. They, too, may benefit from counseling with a child therapist who has expertise in working with loss in children.

Hopefully you will not have to cope with these extreme losses, but during day-to-day deployment, every day can feel stressful and sad. You can help your child feel safe during a deployment separation by maintaining as consistent and routine of a schedule as possible. Make room in your schedule to listen nonjudgmentally to what your child thinks are pros and cons of moving, losing friends, or having a parent deploy. Children under age ten will usually play out their thoughts more than talk them out, so give your children room to play and toys (including a nonrealistic-looking play gun and military-related toys) that they can use to act out their understanding of what the deployed parent is going through. Professional child-centered play therapists usually have a play gun in the room for the children to process their thoughts with. The toys are the children's words, and playing is their language. Video games in general are not therapeutic for loss and trauma because they do not allow for creative expression of one's experience.

> Children should have an opportunity and forum to discuss their own feelings of loss and sadness.

It is not unusual for children to experience guilt for their parents leaving on deployment because in their minds the world revolves around them, so they believe they must have caused the deployment. Children worrying about their parents at work (military training or actual deployment) is normal; they will feel confused about why a deployment is necessary, and a preteen mind will not be able to grasp how long six or eighteen months lasts. Teachers have identified that in a classroom they must often be sensitive to the stressors that young children may be under when they come to class and how much the military child can realistically concentrate on when completing class assignments.

Having a globe or map available to show children where their deployed parents are located can help; keeping abreast of troop movements and keeping a second clock that is set to that deployed parent's time zone can help the child feel more connected to a deployed parent. Children can contribute to care packages sent to deployed parents by submitting their own poems, stories, and drawings.

Violence

If you have seen combat as a parent, you may be somewhat desensitized to the gruesome side of life. Death and killing may not shock you, but to children, these things are still shocking and should remain shocking, at least until they are young adults. Do not make it your job to desensitize them to the shocking nature of violence through exposure to violent movies and video games. Such exposure almost inevitably comes, but hopefully not until they are older and more mature. The sensitive and vulnerable side of children is a strength that helps them see positives in their lives and enjoy simple things that they do have control over. Their tender souls should be protected and cultivated for an increase in compassion and care, which will serve them better in almost every circumstance.

Violent video games and movies may seem like good practice for real life to you as a professional soldier or marine, but to children, they can be difficult or impossible to process in a healthy way. Young minds are not fully processed and view everything in concrete ways. Children are not able to process abstract constructions and violent behaviors viewed in video games and thus distinguish them from real life without an adult discussing it with them in concrete terms. Even twenty minutes of playing a video game has been shown to increase aggressive thoughts and behaviors in humans, while repeated exposure may contribute to the development of more permanent aggressive traits. Preventing exposure to violence is different from acting it out in a play setting with a play gun because in that case children are only acting out what they have already seen and thus are appropriately processing the information.

Slow Is Smooth: Spending Time Together

Consider the time you do have with your children as sacred. They will never be that age again; even the time of one deployment may be the difference between seeing your child as a newborn and returning to see him or her feeding himself or herself. Stephen R. Covey, in the book *The 7 Habits of Highly Effective Families*, reminds us that fast is slow and slow is fast. This paradox is critical in understanding family dynamics, as is the paradoxical statement that big is small and small is big. You can take your kids to Disneyland regularly, but if you are angry and impatient, the "big stuff" is small. Being loving and patient is the "small stuff" that is really big!

Use whatever you can to get to know your children. If they like Pokémon, learn something about Pokémon so you can relate to them. Love is the emotion children most want to be shown and the one they are most apt to feel toward you if you create a context for them to show it. Take time to go on vacation and to have fun with your kids, thus making up for lost time and creating a context for reconnecting with your children. While deployed, hopefully you were able to send small messages to your children (no matter how young) letting them know how much you love and care about them. Now that you're home, keep doing that, and capitalize on new ways to show your love. One father told me that he rarely had time even on the weekdays to be with his newborn son because of his late training and the child's early bedtime, so on weekends he was happy to wake up in the middle of the night so he could spend time feeding him.

Recently, the Flourishing Families project at Brigham Young University concluded that parents who played nonviolent video games with their daughters had daughters who had better behavior, felt more connection to the family, and had stronger mental health. "But wait," you say, "video games rot kids' brains!" Apparently not if they are playing it with a parent. Having said all this now, you may be pulling out the old cliché that it is quality not quantity, but I say it is both quality and quantity. Get in as much of both as you possibly can.

If you decide that your kids don't really need you or your time because they have teachers, friends, and extended family to raise them, there is a chance that you will be disappointed with how these people influence your child. You can't blame another person for how your child turns out if you weren't involved. Perhaps you expected your children to grow up and serve in the armed forces too, but they have zero interest in it because their experiences in the military were you being absent so much and distracted when you were home. It is your responsibility to invest vast amounts of energy into raising your own children, no matter what that sacrifice may cost.

You want your kids to learn independence, but you want to have them learn how to be responsible and mature with their independence and to be safe. You don't want to kick them out of the home too early, and you don't want to make them so dependent that they won't leave, either. When you spend time with your children, you will be modeling mature adult behavior and responsible decision making that they may have the opportunity to learn from no one else.

Rock Climbing and Relationship Building

Developing a positive, trusting relationship with your child is essential for appropriate developmental growth. The relationship will also facilitate your child even wanting to spend time with you. I would compare practical relationship building to rock climbing. If you've ever rock climbed outdoors, you know that some walls appear to be a blank slate. There seem to be no holds and nowhere to put your feet. Your relationship with your child may appear to be impossible and beyond repair; you may believe that it is hopeless to even try. You study the wall and you feel around with your hands until you find one tiny hold that barely contains two fingers, but you pull on it and step your foot into a tiny divot. With your pull of faith, you now see that there is one more spot that you can grab with your left hand that you couldn't see from the ground. Again, you grasp it and find a small spot for your foot. Upwards and onwards, sometimes falling and getting back on the wall with greater concentration, focus, and skill, you don't give up. The aesthetics of climbing are where the joy comes in; reaching the top is only as satisfying as the climb was difficult. Slowly and carefully creating a relationship with your child is a process that you can enjoy along the way.

Don't Be a Drill Sergeant at Home

Drill sergeants are not supposed to have any kind of relationship with their recruits that could resemble a friendship. Parents, though, should have close relationships with their children. The parents should not try to act like their children's peers or encourage poor choices, but they should be emotionally available to connect with their children. A parent friend can be there when the child returns from a first date to talk about how it went. As a parent friend, you can talk with your children about choices they will be facing in the future and listen to their ideas nonjudgmentally.

Apply good leadership that doesn't create fear in your children. Create confidence and independence by developing a relationship in which your child feels safe trying to learn from you and not just trying to guess what your mood is and what you want. Model the behavior you want your child to do. As one father of a five-year-old son shared with me in lament, "My son seems to be doing everything that I do." This particular father had acted abusively toward his wife, and now his son was acting abusively toward him, his son's mom, and his son's sister. I reminded him that if he could train his son to be abusive without even trying, then perhaps, with effort and deliberation, he could actually train his son to be a more kind and loving person by changing his example. The father did just that and found that it made him happier as well and significantly improved his relationship with his son. Fathers have enormous power but often downplay their impact, for better or worse. Kids are sensitive to who has the most power in the home, and they will align themselves with the power to avoid being hurt by the power. Children are always watching and learning.

A drill sergeant gives command, and his or her orders are mission oriented. However, a military parent takes into account the emotions of his or her children and carefully considers how his or her own emotions may impact the entire family. One sergeant father related how after taking some parenting classes he began listening to his three-year-old daughter. He was surprised how sensitive she was to his emotions and

Apply good leadership that doesn't create fear in your children.

to her own emotions when she asked him if she could be sad about a particular family matter. He was speechless and of course encouraged her to feel sad about the loss. By allowing her to feel sad, he realized that he also had much to be sad about himself and was benefitted by her example.

Another corporal father related that after having a history of violence in his home toward his wife, he had become more sensitive to how it was impacting his children. He was surprised by how well and how much his son listened to everything he said. He learned much about how to be more loving in his home and to avoid entitled violence toward anyone in the family. His empathy grew as he actively listened to his child.

A drill sergeant's job is to remove all individuality from the recruits and create a cohesive, exactly-obedient team. A military parent should encourage healthy choices and the development of each child's unique personality. Drill sergeants are instructed to act using extreme measures to prepare recruits for extreme future conditions. I do not encourage any of these extreme methods in the home. Throwing your child's mattress against the wall while yelling in a drill sergeant voice about the filthiness of your child's bedroom can be terrifying to a child. Violent knife-hand movements and spitting in a child's face are not things that children are developmentally capable of handling like an adult, who can differentiate the behavior from the person. To a child, you must be a violent person if that is how you are acting, even if you know that you would never hurt the child. You lose trust when you act in unpredictable and violent ways around children. Hazing in the military is illegal, and any similar behavior in the home is considered child abuse and must be reported.

The goal should be to create a safe environment for your children where they can ask questions, have differing opinions from you, learn responsibility, and learn from mistakes. Unless you are interested in always being in control of your child, even when he or she is at college and working his or her own job, you should start early to encourage independent thinking and acting in your children so that you can launch them successfully into responsible adulthood. After boot camp or basic training, the individual is almost definitely more compliant, but at least some of the individuals that I worked with struggled to remember how to act independently or have their own opinions, which created some issues in their interpersonal lives.

Independent Thought: Military Identity vs. Child's Own Identity

It is important to let kids have their own thoughts, feelings, and emotions. They will fight you tooth and nail to preserve their own thoughts, feelings, and emotions. Active-duty members are told what to wear, how to wear it, how and when to cut their hair, and how to act and respond to almost any given situation; but even with all these controlling outside sources, it is indisputable that each service member has his or her own thoughts, feelings, and emotions, which differ greatly between individuals. Children should be allowed the same privilege; just because they are smaller and you can use a tremendous amount of force and various angles to try and get them to think a certain way does not mean that you should. One service member shared with me that his son's mother kept correcting her young son's sideways hat, and the son kept readjusting it to the side until the mother took it off his head and put it in the backpack. This same father was embarrassed to bring another son on base because of the young man's long hair and nonmilitary bearing.

This is not unique to military parents. Too often, parents tie up their identities with their children's identities. One mother expressed it well when she said that how your kid acts reflects on you. It is true that it does reflect on you, but it isn't who you are, and intelligent observers will be able to recognize the difference between you and your child's preferences. Others will respect you for allowing your children to choose their own appearances, short of blatant immodesty, breaking military dress codes on base, or mutilating their bodies. Some may judge your parenting by what your child wears. If you did your job when they were younger, your children will already know what preferences of dress that you have, and you won't have to lecture them daily on your disapproval. This is an especially sensitive topic because people do identify themselves and others by what clothes they wear. Troops take pride in wearing matching, immaculate uniforms, and it does send a powerful message to observers. How children feel about themselves can change and even improve as they learn to groom themselves well. Often their outer dress is a reflection of inner thoughts about themselves, and your time as a parent may be better spent nurturing your children than shaming them for their appearances.

As a parent, you can and should teach and encourage the discipline of proper grooming to your children, but don't force them with anger. Instead, motivate them with love and have a relationship with them that makes them want to make you proud. If you have a relationship of love, if your children see you dressing well and holding your head high in public, they will usually want to emulate you. Every kid is prone to a period of rebelliousness; recognize it for what it is and continue to love your child for who they are, regardless of his or her peer- and media-influenced appearance. Your love will help your child work through the rebelliousness and back to you.

Do not tell your kids what they are thinking or what they should be thinking. Just because you went through childhood doesn't mean that you know what your child is thinking. The backwards connection involves you assuming that you know people better than they know themselves. Unless you are God, you probably don't, and if you think you do, you're probably wrong. If your kid wants to play a sport, then let him or her try it. Unless you think the child is at high risk of being seriously hurt or that there will be seriously harmful implications for the child, try to allow him or her the freedom to do it. Your child will appreciate you more if you allow him or her independence. At the same time, kids do want stability, and they want to know that you care. Don't say, "I don't care, do whatever you want." Apathy is the lowest state of the body, and your kids need to know that you are putting

> Do let your children know that you care, and ask them lots of questions.

effort into the relationship if they are going to invest their own energy into it. Do let your children know that you care, and ask them lots of questions, like "Why are you interested in that?" Each child is going to be different in his or her identity and requires that you be sensitive and tuned in to what he or she is saying. Listen to the quiet, small things your children say and ask questions. Don't demand your children to listen to everything you say if you aren't going to offer the same respect to them.

Traditions

Children need tradition in their lives. The military is full of tradition and ceremony. The military takes pride in presenting its highest awards to its service members. Recently, a former marine was flown to Washington, DC, so that the President of the United States could present him the Medal of Honor. The award is less important to many than the ceremony and presentation of the award. If the award had been simply mailed to the recipient, it would have been much less meaningful than having it presented with video cameras rolling and journalists present. The process is more important than the content. The ceremony may take significant time to prepare and cost significant amounts of money, but it is worth it to those who understand the value of process.

Children need process. They don't just want to go to Disneyland; they want to go with the family, and they want to buy the goodies and souvenirs because of the memories they evoke. If all that is too expensive, just taking pictures with the family is a tradition that will preserve memories, especially on vacation. I remember as a child seeing an extended family at Disneyland having their picture taken. There weren't just five or six of them; there were probably thirty or more family members each proudly wearing a shirt that displayed, "Family Reunion." As a child, I looked at their broad smiles and wondered why my family didn't have cool shirts that matched like theirs. What may seem corny to you as an adult can be priceless to a child. A tradition can be something as simple as eating dinner together at night or saying grace before eating. The process is not actually eating the food; it is doing it together and sharing time together. Perhaps that is the reason why when two strangers meet and are attracted to one another, the first thing they want to do is eat together. Establish traditions and rituals that make your children feel like they are a part of something bigger than themselves.

Summary

By creating a positive relationship with your children, you may stem off the negative effects of moving, having a parent deploy, transitioning to a new school, and losing friends. Your children are being immersed in a new culture that is military saturated and has no geographical boundaries like the city you may have grown up in. Families who spend time together playing and vacationing are more likely to have positive relationships. Positive parenting includes modeling mature adult behavior and setting limits, thus creating a safe context in which your child can mature into his or her own unique personality. Drill sergeants and drill instructors play an important role in creating excellent service members, but their methods should not be applied to parenting. Good parenting should include encouraging independence, divergent thought, creativity, and individual preference without yelling or forcefully kicking or throwing things around the room. Children naturally love their parents and are anxious to please them and will seek out your attention if you create space and time for them to approach you. If you are a military child, try to appreciate your unique situation and utilize what opportunities life has given you.

How Parents of Service Members Can Help (and Not Help)

Many parents with children who are service members are extraordinarily proud of them and do everything they can to support them morally and verbally in the unique demands of military life. Other parents may want to know how to do this better but have concerns or do not know how. Military Family Central offers ten ways to generally support your deployed adult child. One of my favorites from the list is to keep your thoughts positive (number eight) because your positive thoughts could be what keeps your service member alive and well in a very stressful situation.

Whether your child who is a service member is married or not, as a parent, you are still an important person in your child's life. Let's talk about what your role is if your child is single and enlisted, since most parents still feel at least some responsibility for their child when he or she enlists at age eighteen. With a parent's permission, anyone can enlist to join the armed forces at age seventeen, and at age eighteen, no parental consent is needed. There is a pretty big difference between being an enlisted service member and a commissioned officer. Enlisted service members can start right out of high school but have to meet strict moral, legal, financial, and physical standards. Officers have to meet even more competitive standards and generally join only after completing a college undergraduate degree. Either way, joining the armed forces suggests that you have lived a more exemplary life than the average teenager, the majority of whom are not eligible for service.

You spent your whole life teaching your children. You may have taught them from a distance, absent-mindedly or formally, but you taught them. Now you get to see whether they will choose to apply the principles you taught them. You may even get to see if the principles you taught them were adequate. Principles can be thought of as maps, and if you have the wrong map or if it is lacking important features and contours, you could find yourself walking off a cliff. Sometimes parents are surprised when their children come back to them saying they enlisted specifically because they thought it was what you as a parent would have wanted. Maybe your son joined the Marine Corps because he thought his father would want him to be the "first to fight" and "the few, the proud." Maybe your daughter joined the army so she could "be all that [she] can be," just like you taught her. Some youth run away to join the military because they think they will make their parents proud and "aim high" if they join the US Air Force. Or maybe they want to have cool combat stories to tell, like their parents and grandparents. Some youth join simply because they are patriotic souls that care about the principles of freedom.

Be Proud of Your Child's Choice

As a mother or father of a service member, it is now your duty to morally support your adult child. If your child has not yet made a decision, you may want to take time to help him or her explore options to show your support. If your child already joined, he or she is no longer free to drop out, and anything you do to try and make him or her pay for his or her decision will only reflect poorly on you. If anything, paradoxically, you may drive your child away from you and further towards the military. For example, your son or daughter may decide to take holiday leave and vacation elsewhere with newfound combat buddies if home has become a place where he or she doesn't feel like he or she fits anymore. One navy recruit described online how his parents es-

Love your child unconditionally.

sentially disowned him because joining the military contradicted their religious beliefs. Other parents may disagree with military recruiting because they don't want their kids in combat. If you are at all disappointed in your adult child's decision, take some time to cry in private, but respect your child's independence and love your child openly. If your child excels in the military, and you have respected his or her adult decision, you can only expect honor and respect in return. Pat yourself on the back; your child has made a decision that will potentially make him or her stronger in many ways.

If I could give only one piece of advice to the parents of service members (or even to parents who are service members), it would be to love your child unconditionally. Don't give your child atten-tion only if he or she does what you want for him or her. Do call your child regularly and offer a nonjudgmental listening ear and updates from home. Do care about what your child is doing and really listen to his or her stories; often, service members come into counseling to talk because no one at home seems to care about or appreciate the anguish they have been through recently. At first, I thought I must be hearing them incorrectly; why would anyone not want to hear military stories? But these service members de-scribed how their parents' eyes would gloss over when they tried to describe their training, their friends, and their difficulties. If you remember from an earlier chapter, listening (i.e., empathic listening) means being aware of, understanding of, and sensitive to another's thoughts, feelings, and experiences without judging; to do this effectively, you should probably ask a lot of questions. You may think you don't know enough to even ask a relevant question, but asking questions and giving your full attention to the answers will show that you care. Be sensitive and know that some topics may be uncomfortable to the service member, so try asking in a private, one-on-one conversation rather than at the dinner table or where others could hear. This will allow you to determine sensitivity and avoid embarrassment for both of you.

Perhaps your adult child is stationed several days drive away from you, and you wonder how you will ever serve your parental duties and show your pride in him or her without being able to see him or her directly. You've tried calling, but you usually get the voicemail. You e-mail, but your e-mails go unanswered; your child is probably reading your e-mails or snail mail and appreciating them, but . . . have you tried texting? Most young people in the military text one another. Texting is quiet, and it can be done quickly and without much notice even while service members are working, or it can be done frequently even while they are having a conversation with someone else, like their counselor (as I've observed). Skyping or some other video face time is a popular way to interact among service members.

Mixed Feelings

Let's assume that your son or daughter joined the military, and you have mixed feelings about him or her serving. You love your child, and you are proud of your child. You feel happiness but sadness and fear at the same. Perhaps you would have preferred that your military child had just settled down in the suburbs near your house, lived a simple professional life with little risk, and gave you grandkids to visit regularly. It's time to modify your dream. Perhaps your child joined the military to get away from the fantasies that others had for him or her; maybe your child still loves and cares about you, but he or she wanted to create his or her own independent life. Your child may regret his or her decision when he or she gets on the bad side of an ill-tempered sergeant, but your child wants to make decisions for his or her own self.

Military life and college life both include lots of young, single adults making new decisions that they hopefully learn from. College students regularly die from drunk driving, and so do service members. The inherent risks of military life (e.g., Taliban, Al Qaeda), though, do push the worries of danger a little more to the forefront of one's thoughts. You may wish sometimes that you could "ride shotgun" with your child all the time and protect him or her from the dangers he or she is bound to encounter or be the little angel on your child's shoulder that prompts your child to make or not make certain decisions. If you could, perhaps you would chase off your child's bullies and negotiate your child's salaries and promotions. Maybe you've already tried that when your child was younger, and if so, stop.

Having fears and concerns for your children and regretting some of their decisions while feeling sadness and love for them shouldn't be new for you as a parent. Letting go of them as an adult, though, is a new feeling, and one that is full of mixed feelings which will become clearer as you learn more about what a military choice means.

Consequences and Reinforcers

Consequences and time are the molders of responsibility. Allowing people to suffer their own consequences is good advice for mothers of single or married active-duty family members. A mother and father may not approve of their child's fiancé and warn their child not to marry him or her but later love the new son- or daughter-in-law as much as their own child. Who is to say that your judgment is necessarily better than your child's? You've made poor choices in the past, right? And you learned from those poor choices.

Maybe you would have appreciated someone talking to you about the decision and helping you process each option, but you probably wouldn't have tolerated anyone interfering with your right to decide for yourself. Behaviorally, people generally will do whatever they are rewarded for and not do what they are punished for. The world has a way of shaping people if they are left to suffer natural consequences. Our duty as parents is to warn and exhort, teach, and lead; gradually, we loosen the reins on our youth and allow them more and more freedom. By the time they are adults, we should have them so well educated that we can entirely remove any reigns from them, and they will walk their own safe paths and teach their own children correct principles.

> Our duty as parents is to warn and exhort, teach, and lead; gradually, we loosen the reins on our youth and allow them more and more freedom.

In-Laws

Mothers and fathers worry about their children. That is a good thing. They want the best for their children. They enjoy taking care of their children and seeing them happy. You may be extraordinarily happy to see your child enlisted or commissioned in the armed forces. Perhaps he or she is continuing a family legacy of military service. As the primary nurturer of your children, you would like to believe that they are the best and will always make the best decisions under the circumstances. We want our child's spouse to treat and care for our child the same way that we treated and cared for him or her. Perhaps you are the kind of parent who already joyously supports your adult son or daughter in the military, and you know what a challenge it can be, and you wish that you could be there all the time to help. When this new daughter-in-law or son-in-law is negligent in providing the same care and feeding that you did, you may be disappointed or even angry and disapproving. If the partner of your child is truly being abusive, it is appropriate to intervene and to help your child escape. If not, then you may be the one acting out of line. If your child is the one who's being abusive, don't let him or her off the hook.

Unfortunately, I met many wives of male service members who reported that their mothers-in-law or fathers-in-law did not believe them when they reported abuse. Being a supportive parent does not mean denying culpability of the service member. If all mothers held their sons and daughters responsible for their abusive behaviors, we would have far less abuse in the world — maybe none. Your son or daughter may be a national hero, so encourage them to act that way at home without excuses. Such a service on your part will not only help your son or daughter be happier but also the father or mother of your grandchildren. Those grandchildren will be more likely to continue the legacy of serving their country honorably if they can look to both parents as an example on and off deployment.

The probability is high that if your adult child married someone while he or she was active duty, he or she probably married someone who is not from your hometown. If your child married someone from another country he or she was stationed in, the cultural differences are going to be huge. If your child married someone from another part of the country or even from a different part of the state, the cultural differences are still going to be significant. The differences might be just different enough that you even think he or she is rude and inconsiderate. For example, men and women I interviewed from the southeastern part of the country believed that Californians were rude because they spoke with such forthrightness on certain issues. Californians thought the southeastern people were rude because they avoided issues and were not forthright. In the South, it is polite to refer to adults as "sir" or "ma'am," but on the West Coast it is often seen as rude and sarcastic. The culture of the military itself will actually change your son or daughter significantly, and that is something to consider when you would like to blame the new in-law for changed behavior. In the military, all officers are referred to as "sir" or "ma'am," and topics like death and killing are spoken of with much more frequency and with a directness that some might say is rude and irreverent. Accept the fact that things are different now, and your child is never going to be the same again now that he or she is married and in the military. You can keep your own identity while your child changes his or hers (to fit his or her spouse and service) and still find ways to show love to one another.

My suggestion is to treat the new in-law as if he or she were an honored guest when he or she comes to visit. Avoid making an immediate judgment call based on his or her dress and appearance, because it might just be cultural, and it definitely is what your child likes. Military wives (often referred to as dependents) really are kept dependent in many ways on their active-duty spouse. Frequent moves often prevent them from being able to keep well-paying jobs themselves, and their own educations are often cut short when a PCS (permanent change of station) occurs. Show some respect for son- and daughter-in-laws who sacrifice their own preferences for where they want to live to follow your children. Family members and new in-laws can practically read each other's minds when it comes to knowing whether or not they are being judged. We know if someone is thinking negatively about us or judging us harshly, even when that person is smiling and talking pleasantly. When we do feel like someone dislikes us, we are more likely to judge him or her as well and act reciprocally. The principle that I suggest in interacting with in-laws is to love them, even if they don't love you. Set boundaries for them and for yourself, but love them unconditionally. That does not mean letting them get away with things that you wouldn't let others in the family get away with (unless it was a bad rule to start with). It does not mean enabling them. It doesn't mean necessarily endorsing their beliefs and values, but it does mean appreciating them as humans and as the sons or daughters of someone else. When we think these positive things of other people, they will feel our approval of them as a human being, and if we are patient, they will usually come to appreciate us back.

Deployment Pains

Missing a child can be as painful as missing a spouse. Deployments are heart-wrenching ordeals for everyone involved. Your service-member child will be grateful for anything you send from home with good intentions. Your deployed child will also appreciate positive conversation that isn't centered around how much you miss him or her and wish he or she would come back. Your child wants to know you miss him or her, but it is possible that your child actually enjoys being deployed and experiencing what he or she signed up to do. If he or she doesn't love the deployment, he or she still may not appreciate constantly being reminded of how much you worry about him or her. Listen closely to what your child says and pay close attention to his or her needs. If your child starts talking about his or her deployment, listen closely and ask questions that show your attention. If the child holds back information, it may be because the information is secret and discussing it could put others at risk. Do not encourage your child to divulge any information that might disclose confidential information.

> Your child wants to know you miss him or her.

It is possible that your child is serving faithfully because he or she wants to make you proud or fulfill a legacy. Express your pride often, and encourage your child when he or she is down. Sometimes your child may ask you to contact someone at home and fulfill some special request. If you can fulfill these requests, do so to the best of your ability. If your child is married or has children, your best service may be in comforting the dependent spouse and/or caring for the children. Grandparents regularly take on the responsibility of caring for grandchildren while the single parent deploys or dual military parents deploy. While this may come at a financial cost or considerable investment of all your time and resources at much inconvenience, it may be the closest you get to spending a lot of time with your grandchildren who otherwise might live out of state or country. As a grandparent, you may provide a stable influence in the child's development that will last a lifetime. Such time may also help root the child or children to the hometown that you hope they will eventually return to at some point in the future. Check back on the previous chapter for more tips on helping military children cope with the pains of missing a deployed parent or moving from home.

Systemic Principles of Change

The overriding theme that is ever raised in marriage and family therapy is that you can only change yourself. Nevertheless, paradoxically, it is in changing ourselves that we strongly influence others to change. Consider the metaphor of the watch gears; if a watch has gears that all interact with one another, what happens when I start turning a gear the opposite direction? In the same manner, others must change if we change. Otherwise, they must break while resisting the influential changes or leave.

As a mother or father, it is our obligation to develop and increase our own expressions of love before we can expect love back from our own children, because isn't that what you really want from your child? Love. If you want more than love from your child, perhaps you are being too controlling. Patricia Evans, in her book *Controlling People*, discusses how we too often assign traits to others, and without even asking them, we assume we know them simply by looking at them or because we gave birth to them. Evans continues that this "backwards approach" leads to a "backwards connection" in which someone other than one's own self is defining one's own thoughts, feelings, and traits, which "is only one tiny step away from establishing a control connection." In a controlling connection, the parent or spouse may genuinely believe that he or she knows what is best for the other person and expect him or her to always act in a certain way that fits the parent's or spouse's needs. This illusion may fit what the parent believes is best for the service member, but it rarely is a perfect fit and may in turn lead the service member to act out rebelliously to prove his or her independence.

Service members are taught in their basic training that they are part of a larger team but individually must do what they can to build the team. Young service members have shared with me how much it means to them that their parents love and care about them and that, despite the difficulties they may be having in the service, their parents are thinking of them at home. As a parent, you are extremely influential, and it is your duty to let your child reach his or her full potential. Avoid assigning your own dreams to your child; you taught him or her everything you could to make him or her a responsible citizen and good family member. You may not think that your child should be acting a certain way, but he or she is, and that is evidence that your child has his or her own dreams and own perceptions. Do not assume that you know how your child is supposed to think or feel or that he or she should believe you just because you said something. What you may perceive as your child overreacting may be based on things you can't see or feelings that you haven't taken the time to understand.

You may find that your child has serious fears and doubts about himself or herself that he or she has never been able to express before. Your child may be just as worried about you as you are about him or her. One service member expressed profound sadness when he discovered that his father had been in a serious accident and was facing possible legal charges. This service member was a large, tough veteran with several years in the service, but he could not hold back the tears as he expressed his concern for his family. He was afraid to talk to his family on the phone because he thought he was a disappointment to them.

They were afraid to tell him the details because they knew how it emotionally affected him. There were no easy answers in this situation, and both parties eventually had to patiently listen and comfort one another over long-distance phone calls.

Even if you are a parent who tenderly loves and cares about your child and has always been supportive and proud of your adult child, you have probably still had to make continued changes in your approaches and sometimes revised your hopes and dreams for him or her as things changed. By being sensitive to these changes, you are unburdening your child from having to fulfill your dreams and allowing him or her to live his or her own life and create his or her own dream without having to tiptoe around rigid expectations that may or may not be possible in his or her current situation. Remember, your primary goal is to share in a relationship of love with your children and in-laws; don't let any other fantasies of how they are "supposed to be" get in the way. This will make you more emotionally available and make them more willing to hear your ideas and opinions.

When people are in their twenties, they are weighing in on their lives and deciding for themselves what they're really responsible for. No matter how much you worked to provide a good life for your child, he or she may still blame you and other authority figures for whatever current problems he or she is facing in life and in the military. Your child may say that you should have put him or her in Junior ROTC or that you should have taught him or her how to shoot or how to respect authority or that you should have helped them to get more education. Gradually, however, your children will realize that even if they had a perfect childhood, they still are the only ones responsible for their current decisions, weaknesses, and problems. With time, they will even realize how much you did provide for them and how much worse life would have been without you. Don't give up on your service member. They need you and your nonjudgmental support, not your criticism.

Summary

Lucky you! Your son or daughter is serving his or her country in the military and learning discipline and skills in an unparalleled setting. If you always dreamed of your son or daughter serving his or her country, your services will be most valuable during a deployment, and you can help connect your child to the States through letters, care packages, phone calls, and special requests. Perhaps, however, you didn't dream of your child joining the military or that particular branch, or you didn't dream of your child marrying anyone from a different culture, moving far from home, acting a certain way, or holding certain beliefs. Allow yourself to be sad and to mourn any lost dreams, but now take time to create new visions that include your child in military service. Let your child fulfill his or her own dreams that may or may not coincide perfectly with yours. Be an adult when dealing with your adult child; be as emotionally mature as you hope your child will be. Be as respectful of his or her decisions as you would like him or her to be of yours. Carefully analyze the hopes and dreams that you have for your adult child and consider whether these dreams leave room for your son or daughter to make his or her own decisions. Be appropriately emotionally available to your children when they come to you for counsel. Avoid telling them how they *should* act. Instead, consider how a wise friend might help support or gently walk another friend through the various options of a difficult decision—even if you think you already know what the right decision might be. In the end, wait for your adult child to ask for your opinions rather than just jumping in. If there have been breaks in trust between you and your child, you may have to wait a long time to gain that trust again, but be available without resentment during that time while you both learn about life in the modern US military.

Gearing Up for Deployment

Dear Service Member,

You've got a million things to prepare for before you leave, but you've been training for these final days for months or years. You will do fine on deployment, but what about your family? They've been reading this book, and hopefully they understand a little better about how to respond to you and your needs, and you understand how to be more sensitive to them. You're both sacrificing for one another, and you are both dreading the distance that deployment will put between you. Maybe you've already deployed and you have an expectation of how it will be. How can you be sure that while you are deployed the kids will be OK and your spouse will continue to be faithful to you? How do you know you aren't going to do something you'll regret or act in a way that you wouldn't if they were there with you?

Feed the Relationship

You can't control what your partner or kids do, but you can control what you do, and you can educate yourself and perhaps your partner. The risk is real (and high) that you will do things you don't want your partner to know about. Affairs while partners are deployed are common, as are bad financial decisions, giving in to other unhealthy behaviors, and succumbing to enormous stress levels that may give way to deep depression. A marine told me once that an affair is doing something you wouldn't want your partner to find out about. Would your partner feel disappointed, sad, heartbroken, or betrayed if he or she knew how you were talking to another person? The time to prevent an affair is now, before anyone leaves on deployment—not when you're staring into the eyes of some other attractive person and thinking about what you could do.

Avoid anything that could possibly compromise you. Don't ride alone in a car with someone of the opposite sex, don't talk to someone of the opposite sex on the phone or in person about intimate topics, don't text, chat, or e-mail the opposite sex except for business, don't invite someone of the opposite sex over to your house alone to chat, and don't visit racy websites or tantalize yourself with personal ads. Strengthen yourself now to facilitate the results that you want later. An American Indian once dreamed of two dogs; one was emaciated but appeared kind and friendly, and the other was strong and vicious. The dreamer only had so much food to give the dogs. As he told the story of his dream, listeners asked, "Which one will live?"

"The one I feed," replied the dreamer.

We only have so much energy and time to invest. Teenagers or tweens may say that they have energy to go around, but ultimately, it is not enough to keep both dogs alive. If we invest everything in our marriage, it will live. The problem is that you can't diversify like in stocks and bonds: it's all or nothing. Partners can essentially read our minds and hearts and tell when we're thinking about someone else or when we're trying to hide something. Your own conscience will eat you from the inside out. Service members who think they will keep their affairs a secret divulge early or are found out by their partners. The guilt festers and, like an infection or a parasite, can begin to sap your energy and kill your relationship.

Embezzling from the Relationship

When you invest your intimate energy into another person besides your committed partner, you are essentially embezzling from the marriage. You and your partner share a joint emotional bank account that you make emotional deposits into regularly with good, trustworthy behavior. If you are taking from the account by secretly fantasizing about someone else, you're stealing emotional energy that could have been invested in your family. When people embezzle from a relationship, they usually take a few bucks here and there. At the end of the day when they're counting things up, they make excuses for where the money went, but the bosses or business partners start watching them closely. The thief will often become increasingly brazen in his or her work and eventually take too much, and then the thief is caught! Trust is gone, and he or she is taken off the joint account until he or she can prove himself or herself worthy. In my experience, injured partners may spend years waiting for evidence of trustworthiness before they are willing to cosign on any significant emotional investments with their partner again.

Prevention of Problems

Spend time now nurturing your marriage, and train for the separation from your partner as if it was every bit as important as being mission ready. Go to CREDO (Chaplains Religious Enrichment Development Operation—a weekend marriage retreat through the military), go to FOCUS (Families OverComing Under Stress) or ACS (American Community Service) Resilience Academy in the Army, talk to your chaplain or ecclesiastical leader, or talk to a marital counselor to strengthen your marriage as much as possible. The problem is that research shows the more a partner is deployed, the more his or her marriage suffers. You might get better at knowing what to expect and handling the stresses of deployment better, but you are missing valuable time together that could have been spent bringing you closer together. That absence and distance makes huge withdrawals from the emotional bank account of strength that you have been so carefully building up for the deploy-

> Take the opportunity to grow stronger as an individual and learn all you can about correcting unhealthy relationship problems.

ment. That isn't a bad thing; you will just have to prepare yourself by making big investments now to compensate for it as much as possible. Deposits and withdrawals from your relationship bank account are normal and should be expected. Sometimes you might feel rich with trust and fondness, and other times you may be in debt. Therefore, you need to build up an emotional reservoir of strength, as much as possible, before you leave. Go on vacations together without the kids or in-laws, go on a date (just the two of you) every week, or have more pillow talk.

Unfortunately, I have yet to hear a couple tell me that a deployment has helped their marriage grow stronger. I have heard women say that they realized they felt more independent and healthier while their husbands were deployed, and some have even realized that they felt safer while their husbands were deployed and became conscious of unhealthy patterns that existed when their husbands were home. Some of these women took the opportunity to grow stronger as individuals and learn all they could about correcting unhealthy relationship problems; some took the time to separate and divorce. If you are in a healthy relationship, you can at least use the time to become more skilled in relationships and communications and motivated to work on your marriage.

You may think your marriage is pretty strong right now, and you may see the deployment as just a short time apart that you will survive. If so, that's a positive way to think, and keep it up, but in itself, deployment more often than not exposes problems, rather than resolving them. In other words, I wouldn't recommend that someone go on deployment to help his or her newfound love or to repair a troubled marriage. The deployment itself is not a bad thing, but like any other trial, it is a catalyst that can initiate drastic changes: it can stimulate you to work harder and grow stronger or it can sink you. Listen to your spouse and find out what his or her fears are *without* trying to fix them. Too often people (men especially) try to fix problems as soon as they hear about them, but what people often need is a listening ear, not an interruption of why their fears are irrational or how they should be feeling. Spend as much time together as you possibly can while you can, get as close to and intimate with one another as you possibly can, and build as many positive memories and as much loving nostalgia as you can. These memories and positive connections can help get you through the geographical separation without creating a relationship separation.

Nondeploying spouses fear that their partners won't come back alive and that they will mess up the finances (e.g., spend too much, create debt), not be able to handle things on their own, be lonely, not be able to communicate or share important things, or upset and worry the service member so he or she can't focus. Deployed spouses should expect these rational fears and many other seemingly irrational ones from their partners. What are you worried about happening while you or your partner deploys? Make a list of your own and your partner's fears now.

Prepare yourself mentally while your partner is present to handle potentially difficult situations. Bulwark your life against negative outside influences, and stay away from situations that could be compromising and detrimental to your marriage and family. I would even recommend family counseling of some kind to discuss your unique situation. If after doing everything you can to prepare for deployment you still feel a sense of dread, try turning the dread into excitement. Dread is usually a result of un-processed anxiety or fear. Try instead to live in the now and gather up your energy to be fully present as you prepare to live through the challenges of deployment!

Fears, Sadness, and Other Difficult Emotions

Emotions run high when a deployment is on the horizon; you can see the deployment far off in the distance, and as it gets closer, you can either deny its encroachment or face the real feelings of sadness and fear that it brings. If you could have a miracle, what would have to happen to help these fears be alleviated? What can you do right now to prevent these fears from becoming a reality? Ask yourself these questions to identify small steps you can take to prepare for the difficult times that occur in the build up for a deployment. Military families regularly shared with me how the time building up to a deployment is more difficult than the deployment because of the long training weeks, the chaotic prepa-rations, and the anxiety of awaiting the day of departure.

Fears can paralyze us and create extreme anxiety; if the anxiety is not alleviated, it can lead to hopelessness and then depression. Fears are often indicators of deeper-lying emotions. Anxiety is often closely associated with anger, and together these type A feelings lead to a block up of emotions. The months before a deployment (building up to a deployment, as they say) are dif-ficult and full of confusing emotions. Notice each emotion as it comes and take time to process the emotion as it comes. You may feel as though you do not have time for this process because of all the work that must be done. I would suggest that, in this case, you may have time but aren't sure what is necessary to do the processing and even are fearful of how deep the emotion goes. Have faith in yourself and go deep; first, find a safe place to do it, and I would recommend finding a professional counselor.

Let's practice processing right now by using an example. Imagine you just found out that your family member is leaving avant-garde, meaning he or she will be leaving a month or two earlier than everyone else in the battalion. The crunch for time now becomes a double crunch. One of my friends actually had this experience and had to cancel a long-planned trip to Hawaii that was going to be like a honeymoon, since military service had prevented her and her husband from having a honeymoon immediately after their marriage.

Fortunately, my friend who lived far from her family of origin was very capable of adapting, had good friends, and was able to talk it out with friends, family, and her husband. She talked about the sacrifice she was making for her husband to leave, how unfair it felt, how much she wanted to change things, how proud she was of him, how she was glad she didn't have to do it, how she was scared for him, and how she was still going to Hawaii one day! The range of emotions she went through was exhaustive during his full deployment as more and more unexpected things occurred. While she wouldn't wish to go through the experience again, she is a stronger person for having lived through it. The time she invested in processing her emotions in a healthy manner actually made her life more positive. Really, what other options did she have to help her with emotions? Her other options were negative ones, like mood-altering substances and other addictive behaviors that could be used to temporarily escape the pain but ultimately compound the suffering with new problems on top of the preexisting ones.

Marie Angela, a blogger and columnist, wrote about how the sadness and loneliness of deployment never became easier but that she has learned to appreciate various aspects of the experience, including independence, trips with the kids, and friendship with other milspouses (as she calls them). Her own first deployment experience followed a PCS that happened so quickly that her husband left before their household goods arrived in the move. Moving, finding new friends, coping with a toddler, and missing a family member all combined to create an extreme life experience. Sadness and real sorrow do occur because of the separation of deployment, but ignoring these emotions and burying them beneath anger and anxiety may keep them from healing. Grief and sorrow really do hurt physically in our bodies, even without any physical injury; however, like a physical injury, they need exposure. A common clinical observation is that a physical wound needs to bleed and needs oxygen exposure in order to facilitate healing. Allow your emotional wounds to heal by leaving room to cry, grieve, and feel lonely. These emotions, like bleeding, may facilitate the deeper healing of your heart and mind. Sadness itself, if left to occur in an open and accepting way, has an amazing way of binding itself up. The sadness tends to do its healing work primarily within the confines of the heart. Then find time to rejoice and let yourself find happiness, even if it feels like a betrayal to an already sad soul. Whether you are a wife, husband, brother, mother, sister, niece, uncle, or friend to the deploying loved one, you will feel some sense of sadness as he or she departs. Embrace the sadness and enjoy it! This sounds like a contradiction, but as I will discuss in a later chapter, sadness is an absolutely necessary emotion that cleanses the soul.

Caring and Worrying

There is a big difference between telling someone to stop caring and telling someone to stop worrying. You ultimately want to keep caring but stop the worrying through appropriate processing. There are three main steps to coping with worry. The first step is to identify each of your worries. Write each of them down so you can see them. You can do this in private if you are concerned someone will ridicule your worries.

In step two, you should identify what is motivating you to have each of these worries. Usually, the motivating emotion is caring, but it tends to get drowned in fear. Therefore, if you write fear, you should go deeper and recognize underlying emotions, like caring about your own well-being and those of your family. Processing worry, if done with a high level of caring, is good for your soul. Eliminating worry will ultimately leave more room for joy, happiness, and deeper caring—the highest energy states of the body. To not care would be apathy, the lowest energy state of the body.

> Keep caring but stop the worrying through appropriate processing.

Caring will help you focus on step three, which is identifying what emotions would arise if your deepest worries came to pass. Doing this will help you make the connection between your emotions and rational thought. Recent research on the brain has discovered that when people are making personal, rational decisions, a part of the brain called the ventromedial frontal lobe, which governs emotions, lights up with activity. By allowing yourself to consider your worst fears in the context of how they will emotionally affect you, you are actually engaging the parts of your brain that will lead to the most rational decisions. Sadness will probably be one of the most prominent emotions that you would experience in a worst case scenario. Allow yourself to feel sad even thinking about what could happen. Listen to what these emotions can teach you about yourself and how profound your familial relationship is to your existence. Accept the emotions, and let yourself feel them.

Step four is identifying what you would need in your life if you had to work through these very emotions in the event that a worst-case scenario occurred. This step can take some footwork because you may have to do some research. Your deployment may have unique risks that only you know about, and maybe only people in your field could possibly know how best to cope with those specific problems. Find people who have actually had these problems or something similar to them and talk to them and family members that were affected by the problems. Not worrying shouldn't include you sitting at home and just taking it easy like Bob Marley (without a care in the world). It should be an active, preventative approach that includes making preparations and gaining knowledge so that the worries decrease. Allow yourself to feel the grief you would feel if a worst-case scenario occurred, and picture how you would need to work through the emotions that would accompany such a situation. Decide what would be your responsibilities and whose help you would rely on most when processing the losses.

Overall, take preventative steps to minimize and eliminate risks to your physical safety where possible, and learn everything you can about staying emotionally and physically healthy. Doing so will ease the worries of separation during deployment. Worry is a part of our society's mindset, but it can be appropriately worked through and can motivate you to greater action and preparation. The problem comes when you are only worrying and not acting, which is a common form of emotional paralysis wherein you should consider professional counseling. Hopefully, as you work through potential worries and arrive at rational decisions and plans, it will be the only time you have to do this difficult processing for those specific worries. If not, repeat the steps again with more introspection and increased research. Repeat these steps with new worries.

Deployment Support Services

If you are a nondeploying spouse, you should consider joining a spouses group; many of these groups are local and specific to a particular base. In the navy and marines, they have L.I.N.K.S. (Lifestyles, Insights, Networking, Knowledge, Skills), a program in which you can ask more mature members for help, learn about the details of being a military family, ask how the Marine Corps works, and make friends. The Marine Corps is unique in having a FRO (Family Readiness Officer) who works with the battalion commander to coordinate family readiness programs and can be identified online and contacted by phone or e-mail with questions. The army has a Mobilization and Deployment program, and most bases have social organizations for spouses or specifically wives of deployed soldiers. A search on the Internet will help you identify local meetings for family members at your base.

Family-oriented financial programs on base are intended to help families get their finances in order before, during, and after deployment. Look online for your base or fort's local Internet site, and find the tab that identifies family resources; usually there is a whole department of civilian employees whose only goal is to help dependents find solutions. Identifying key resource people on the base will help you feel more comfortable with and less fearful about asking for help before, during, and after deployment. Don't be afraid to ask for help and to introduce yourself to everyone. If a member of your family has a physical or mental disability of some kind, be sure to register with the Exceptional Family Member Program (EFMP) so that the commanders can be sensitive to your needs when considering relocation and deployments. Take a day or two to walk and drive all over the base and get to know what resources are available and where to find them. Pick up brochures on the way that you can refer to later. What isn't a problem could become a problem later, and some of these departments may have proven preventative methods for you to implement.

The military is full of acronyms, hierarchies, divisions, equipment, and procedures that you can't really appreciate without taking time to study them. Don't be afraid to ask what words mean. As the deploying family member, you should make every effort to explain every military procedure you can to your family. Help your family feel comfortable on the base and prepared for possible problems while you are deployed. Be sure to give your partner access to enough money to live (refer to the chapter on finances and local base sources for more information about preparing financially for deployment). Knowing your family is knowledgeable and has access to resources should help you to deploy without worry.

Live It Up before You Deploy!

I once had it explained to me that there are at least four major ways that families deal with problems, and one of them is to go on vacation and have a good time spending money and doing whatever pops into mind. If you come from a family in which vacations were unheard of, you may think vacations are a waste of money, but wholesome recreational activities are good for your family, and that time spent vacationing as a family is a lot cheaper ($1,180 in 2012 for the average vacation) than a divorce (uncontested $1,500; contested $15,000). If you go on a vacation, try to leave the work at home. When your active-duty partner goes on predeployment leave, he or she may still have to be available by phone, and interruptions may prevent the deep solitude that you need. You will have to get creative and enjoy the time that you do have when the phone isn't ringing. One of my friends solved this by not answering his phone; if you're brave enough to do that, it might be a good idea for you, too. Taking a vacation out of state will at least keep the unit from calling an active-duty family member back in the office while on leave. However, vacations do not have to be expensive to be memorable; you don't have to go to an amusement park or to a faraway place. Children often recall that their favorite vacations were in their own backyards when mom and dad came out to play with them for a few hours. Maybe the "backyard" includes a nearby city or a nearby national or state park (with no cell phone reception) to enjoy nature; that kind of vacation may allow you to sleep in your own bed at night, and you can at least turn your brain on vacation mode. I know it's nice to save up your vacation so you can use it for terminal leave at the end of your enlistment or commission, but if you're doing that, be sure to use the vacation days they do give you that include all of the federal holidays like Columbus Day and Veterans Day. These holidays usually include part of the Friday before and part of the Tuesday after the holiday. If you are like many of my friends, taking leave is tricky because your command keeps telling you to take it, but when you request it, your command says he or she can't spare you. Solve this by going when everyone else is taking leave, too, like during predeployment leave.

I'm not suggesting that you go in debt to enjoy yourself before deployment, and I'm not suggesting that you live it up by getting drunk. I am suggesting that you find some creative ways to live it up with your family. Spend time talking to your kids and doing fun things with your spouse and siblings. Go visit your grandparents and extended family so they can show their pride in your service. Many a service member has returned from being home with glowing reports of how family and friends treated him or her like a hero in his or her hometown. Some service members were put in parades, others had meals bought for them, and others were invited to speak to groups and inspire kids. Avoid situations and news that will demoralize you or make you doubt yourself.

Create Memories

There is a real possibility that you may not return from deployment, and you may want your children and spouse to remember you fondly. Take lots of pictures and record yourself on video or audio so family members can listen to your voice and remember how much they miss you. There are resources on base that will film you reading your children's favorite books. My kids' friends had dolls that they could carry with them that included a large picture of their deployed father on the dolls. They carried the dolls with them everywhere they went.

Make Plans

Finally, my recommendation is that you make plans of what the nondeployed family member(s) will do during the deployment. I would recommend that you set aside Sunday night (or some other night) as a family council night, talk about what you are going to do that week, and then look at the long term and discuss what you're going to do during the months or years that your partner is deployed. You can make a list of all the things you ever wanted to do, like sky dive, scuba dive, or learn cosmetology and decide how much time and money each activity will require and by what date you want to do it. Plan what activities you want the kids to be engaged in during the deployment. If you plan to remodel the house, break it down into lots of small steps that are doable and decide how much time you will need to spend in planning these things. When making this list, make it flexible to accommodate for the craziness you may feel as a practically single parent or single person while your partner is deployed. Plan for what problems might come up and how you will handle them; have plan A, plan B, and backup plans if you can. Recognize that none of these plans may work, and you may have to wing it because there are always surprises. If you have your list of things to do, you may be so busy that the time passes faster than you expected.

> Plan for what problems might come up and how you will handle them; have plan A, plan B, and backup plans if you can.

Graveside Wishes

Talk to the deploying family member about what his or her wishes are if he or she dies or is seriously disabled. This discussion may be hard to bring up, but in the end, it will take away the feelings of taboo and take away the fear of the unknown. Talking about graveyard plans or cremation can help. Sometimes in marriages, the partner of the service member and the in-laws don't see eye to eye. Maybe one of them wants the service member buried in his or her hometown and the other wants him or her buried locally or cremated. The service member should make his or her desires known to everyone so there is no mistake. The potential for contention after death or a serious injury and the decision of the division of assets and money are huge. Deciding ahead of time what you will do in the face of death or disability will help prevent contention and allow everyone space to grieve without resentment.

Summary

If at all possible, you should make every effort to prepare yourself for any possibility during the deployment. Process your worries using the steps outlined in this chapter, keep a caring disposition to prevent overanxiety, and find the energy to act. Spend as much time together as you can as a family doing things that enhance your relationships, like vacations and day trips. Such time spent together will help strengthen you against potential infidelity in your marriage and contribute to positive emotions in all of your family relationships. Military bases of any significant size will have many family services available to support family members while their service member is deployed. Get to know each of these services and where they are located at the military station. Difficult emotions, like sadness and loneliness, will arise during a deployment, and their presence should be acknowledged and accepted and learned from. These emotions are not bad in themselves and can actually contribute to a more full appreciation of the depth of your overall human experience that includes loss and temporary loneliness. Worrying is natural in difficult situations, but preparing yourself to deal with tough times will reduce the fear. Finding positive things to do while your family member is deployed will help you to pass the time and expand your awareness and skills. The reality that your family member could die is a sobering truth, and one that should be prepared for and discussed, or even written down. The months leading up to a deployment are difficult and filled with unexpected experiences that you will have to adapt to by processing the accompanying emotions of frustration, disappointment, and surprise. Ultimately, every moment that you can spend appreciating the present and preparing for the future will make the actual deployment less distressing. Family members will appreciate service members who help them learn as much as they can about what will happen during the deployment, and service members will sleep more restfully knowing that their families are prepared back at home.

In-Country (on Deployment) and At-Home

Remember when you and your partner first started dating and you couldn't stand being apart for even a minute? You gazed longingly at every photo, dreaming of that person. Remember how your heart ached for that other person? It was almost a good feeling, and it made you want to be a better person for your partner so that when you were reunited, he or she would love you more. Your partner is now deployed, and maybe you cry yourself to sleep at night and off and on throughout the day because missing your partner is so much harder than you thought it would be. You did everything you could to prepare for the deployment, but there is still a deep ache and emptiness inside of you. That ache is your body's way of expressing its sorrow and sadness. Be glad that your body misses and loves your partner so much.

Wanting to Deploy

Most of the male active-duty service members that I have spoken to have secretly (or openly) expressed their desires to deploy, but to some spouses this feels like betrayal. Often, the service members signed up to deploy, and they want to be in combat. In some ways, life is simpler when you are deployed: you eat your food and you do your duty, which is whatever command tells you to do. However, service members always acknowledge that deployments are sometimes lonely. They do miss their families and they do miss home-cooked food. One marine surprised me when he expressed what he thought were most marines' desires: to talk only about home when they are deployed and on the phone. He said that he didn't want to talk about what was happening in-country (the country he was deployed to); he just wanted to hear about his family, and he did not want to talk about what was happening around him. He wanted to take his mind off the stresses of combat and feel nostalgic about home. Each service member is unique, and deployment will be unique to each of them, so ask your deployed service member what he or she wants to talk about and then listen.

Nondeployed Family Member

If you are the nondeployed family member, you may want to actually hear about what is happening in-country. Be sensitive to the deployed member and know that he or she may not want to talk about what is happening. Being without your family member is emotionally draining. You should take time to be sensitive

> You will be a better parent if you take care of yourself.

to your own sadness, loneliness, and feelings of loss. Take time to pamper yourself occasionally. As discussed in a previous chapter, this does not include reckless abandon, although you could give yourself an allowance and then pretend like you're spending it recklessly to create the same feeling of freedom. Have you ever gone to the spa, gotten a deep massage, or soaked in natural hot springs? If you have kids, do you set aside some money to pay a babysitter so you can go do something you enjoy? If you're trying to save money, have you tried finding someone to trade babysitting with? I believe almost every military base has childcare available at a fairly low cost per child. One wife had her husband deployed three times in three years; she would have gone crazy if she had to care for her four young children alone. She took advantage of the childcare services and went to the gym, learned to golf, went shopping, and spent time with friends or just time alone at home reading a book. I would compare this to putting on your own oxygen mask when it falls from the plane ceiling before you put it on your child's face. You will be a better parent if you take care of yourself.

One young mother with an active-duty husband said she preps her young son for deployments by discussing how Daddy is leaving to "fight the bad guys," reminding him that Daddy loves him, and frequently showing him photos of Daddy. Helping adolescent children believe that their deploying parents are contributing to a good cause is strongly predictive of them coping well while parents are deployed. To a child, a deployment of even a few months can be enough to interrupt his or her attachment with you. Already having a strong family with good relationship boundaries and connections will help kids make it through even multiple deployments. If you are the deploying parent, don't neglect to write and contact home as often as possible, and send photos if it won't compromise the mission.

Love Yourself, Love Your Life

The principle of putting on your own oxygen mask first is that you need to take care of yourself as a military family member or even as the deployed partner; you aren't doing anyone a service if you neglect your own needs and have to be hospitalized for anxiety. Pay attention to when you need physical help; get enough sleep, eat healthy, exercise, and get medical attention or massages when you need them. Stress, depression, and sleep problems are more frequent among deploying and nondeploying spouses while their partners are deployed, so give yourself some credit. Don't beat yourself up if you don't get everything done. Don't try to keep a perfect house or be the perfect partner. Love yourself for who you are—a person with value that your deployed family member loves. You don't have to make life any harder for yourself when your partner is deployed; you don't have to go out and get a job, remodel the house, spend hours volunteering, or take your family on energy-consuming expeditions unless you feel like it will ultimately lower your distress and increase your eustress (good stress). If you aren't sure, then give it a try. Ask friends how they make it work for them.

> Love yourself for who you are—a person with value that your deployed family member loves.

Activities

Everyone is different, and what specific activities you do to enjoy your life are probably less important to pay attention to than your mindset while you do them. If some activities actually make you feel better, contribute to positive thinking, and facilitate processing difficult emotions or keep you from going crazy, keep doing them. However, take time to distinguish between pleasure and practicality; don't participate in activities that could turn into addiction and send you into a negative spiral (e.g., debt, drugs, alcohol, late nights, extramarital affairs).

A good social network full of positive-minded friends will keep you motivated and enjoying life even when you feel like crying.

Finding friends on a military base can take some practice. Seek out people with similar backgrounds as you and then keep asking them to do things with you. If you have children, get to know their friends' parents and invite them to do some fun things with you. Some military mothers believe that their best social networking time is while they are at their children's sports activities because they already have to be there. If, however, driving kids to activities is just energy consuming and not energizing, stop doing it until mom or dad is back in town. You may be the friend that someone else needs to keep them from crying all day, so get out and find others with whom you can talk and discuss your problems. Finding a professional counselor or a chaplain may be a good option if you need someone to discuss things with in confidentiality or need an immediate self-esteem boost and reminder of your value. The DSTRESS hotline (1-877-476-7734) is open twenty-four hours a day, seven days a week and has people available to chat with you about anything you like, including missing a family member.

Spiritual Attendance

You may find yourself struggling spiritually while your partner is deployed, especially if something bad happens to your partner or something potentially bad seems possible. You may find yourself questioning God and wondering why there is so much evil in the world. These are normal feelings. Everyone has a spiritual side, even if they don't have a religious side.

The spiritual side is the one that allows you to love other people and miss them. Spirituality can be found by taking a stroll in nature, pondering why the sky is blue, or meditating in a sacred edifice or at a cemetery. The spiritual part of yourself is the one that you can't see, and science can't define it; yet you feel connections to others and the world around you. I have found in my counseling that most people want to talk about their spiritual experiences, which may include prophetic dreams or deep sadness from missing a loved one or questions about God. Talking to a chaplain on base can be helpful for military family members to process their spiritual ponderings. If you find a chaplain or some other ecclesiastical leader that you disagree with, find another one that is more understanding and provides more insight or a different perspective. If you choose to attend a church, you may find that it provides a social outlet where you can make friends and express emotions to others with similar beliefs going through similar problems. They may have found creative solutions that you hadn't considered.

Whether you are living on or off a base, you can fulfill your spiritual needs by seeking out spiritual texts (every bookstore has a section), talking to people that you are spiritually attracted to, finding a group (or religious organization) that encourages discussion of people's spiritual sides, and finding time to reflect alone in silence. I would encourage you to write in a journal what thoughts and impressions you have from the spiritual side of yourself.

To Stay or Go

Nondeployed spouses may have the dilemma of whether to stay at the duty station or to return to their homes of origin when their spouses deploy. This second option is usually one that only young spouses with little or no children and no career will seriously consider. If you know other people who have deployed, talk to them about the pros and cons. In many cases, you will do better to stay near the base. There, you will have opportunities to connect with others going through similar trials, and you will be able to mature, grow, and develop new coping skills that you wouldn't develop in your hometown. Your parents, family members, and childhood friends may want to understand what you're going through but just don't, and they may make recommendations that aren't in your best interest. If your deployed partner is planning to make the military his or her career, deployments may be a frequent occurrence. If so, you should strongly consider learning the rules of adapting to a deployment now by staying on base so that later when you have kids and a career, you will already have a strong skill set.

Consider making wherever you live your home. If you haven't already done so, tour the town and get to know all the nooks and crannies. If possible, introduce yourself to the librarian, the mayor, all your neighbors, and the other active-duty members and their families within your unit of service. Develop new hobbies and pastimes that are specific to where you live, and visit historical sites that you might otherwise never have seen. Don't just tell yourself that you'll soon be moving so it's no use getting to know anyone. The branches of service are not so big that you won't run into some of these same people again later on. The more people you know, and who know of your needs, the more likely it is that you will be able to receive service from them and provide service for them yourself.

Serving people around you may help you come out of your shell and worry less about your own condition and more about others. It could be something small like

> Consider making wherever you live your home.

taking the neighbor's kids to the park when you take your own kids or calling your neighbors just to see how they are doing or bringing over some home-baked goods on holidays.

Some deployments may be to other countries that allow for the whole family to come if they desire. I have yet to meet someone from a family that went overseas and then regretted it. The cultural submersion alone was worth it for most of these families. They regularly talk about how fantastic it was for their children to attend school and tour other countries and how much it opened their eyes to the rest of the world.

Stay in Touch and Stay Busy

"Try and stay busy" was the advice of one nondeployed spouse. Join programs and have fun! Write lots of letters to your deployed family member and, if possible, Skype and e-mail regularly with your partner. Another nondeployed partner suggested that you write down *everything* that happens daily at home; she wrote what came in the mail, doctor's appointments, and if she had a manicure or got her hair done. She let her deployed husband know what the kids did every day and any developmental steps they made. Then she would send the entire journal to her partner. This helped her deployed partner not feel so left out or as if he were "missing puzzle pieces" when he returned. He told her that it made him feel as if he fit right in when he returned because he knew of small changes in schedules and thinking.

Branch Out for Support

Humans don't do well in isolation; they tend to get a little crazy when they are cut off or cut themselves off from others. Without your deployed family member, it may feel like you are lost and that you have lost your main connection to the world. You may feel little will to live, be creative, or even talk to others. You may just be hoping that if you buckle down and count the days that you'll somehow survive. Don't do it! Pull out the list you made before your partner deployed of all the things you were going to do while he or she deployed and start doing them. It might include visiting tourist areas, learning to crochet or juggle, teaching yourself computer programming, golfing, or practicing tai chi and yoga. Make a schedule to self-improve that isn't over-burdensome, and don't set your expectations so high that you disappoint yourself.

Creative Outlets

If you didn't make a list of things you want to do, do it now. Turn off the TV; that may only be contributing to negative feelings and depression. I would suggest that at least one of the activities be a creative outlet. For example, learn a new musical instrument or genre of music, teach yourself to paint, learn to cook new, exotic foods, write a fictional book, learn sculpturing or scrapbooking or bouquet making. By participating in a creative activity, you will be satisfying and releasing in your body the hormones and neurotransmitters that have to do with fantasy and creativity. As a spouse, you may find that participating in these safe and uplifting creative activities satisfies urges and desires that you might otherwise only satisfy with your spouse present. Do not worry about whether or not you are good at the creative process or if it pleases anyone else. You can throw away your artwork immediately afterwards or keep it for only your eyes. The point is to create. Humans are meant to create, and everyone is capable of participating in this process.

Relax

The next area of your life that you should satisfy is finding a way to relax. This might include sitting in a bath with aromatic candles and bath salts or listening to relaxing music at the end of the day and practicing meditation. In today's world of rush, there is little time set aside for relaxing. If you have kids, put them to bed early and make relaxing a priority.

True relaxation should include creating a greater association with the world around you. By associating yourself, you are connecting yourself with the world around you. Standing or sitting in the grass will help your body to reenergize in a calming way. Pet your dog or cat and talk softly to it; this causes you to release oxytocin (the love hormone), and it lowers your blood pressure. Journal all of your thoughts and feelings to help your brain and body process all the struggles you had through the day. By writing things down, you are actually connecting the dots in your body and mind and making sense out of all that you experienced. If you want to write down things that you would never want anyone else to read, write it on scratch paper and get it all out, then shred it

In my observation, a lot of TV watching is common among those who are depressed, and it only feeds judgmental opinions of yourself and others. Even surfing the Internet for hours and staring at a screen can lead to negative moods not unlike a withdrawal from a drug addiction You may argue that you're different and it relaxes you, and I would agree if it is done in moderation for only an hour or two a day without commercials. Huge problems occur when TV becomes a means of coping with life in general and an entire day or night or week is spent vegging in front of the television. My personal conclusions are that most television shows and their commercials are designed to create anxiety, fear, and shame in their viewers. Peter Koerner writes of similar conclusions:

> Many of you have already figured it out: television creates stress—period. Commercial television is designed and intended to create stress for the simple reason that stressed-out people buy things to sedate or distract themselves—or to solve the problems the television tells them they have. This form of mass-hypnosis has been so effective, there are now thousands of television channels; and, a new mass-market has been generated by creating unrealistic self-images and low self-esteem with artificial images of artificial people—and the answer to your problems just a toll-free telephone call away (and "just three-easy payments of $49.95. . . .").

When we stare at the TV, we are actually going into a state of minor hypnosis (dissociation) and sometimes to such a large extent that we forget how the time passed or what happened. This dissociation is disconnecting; it detaches you from reality. This is opposite from the practice of associating as we discussed at the beginning of this section. Reading books and magazine articles stimulates and relaxes your mind in a less anxious way than TV by making your mind create its own images based on the words which have to be processed and assimilated.

Stimulation and Excitement

Even if you are not an athlete and you don't like taking risks, you can still find ways to energize yourself no matter where you live. Consider getting a Wii and doing the Wii Fit video game for some real fun by yourself or with the kids. There are gyms on every base, and they have programs for everyone. A calendar of yoga, Pilates, Zumba, and other athletic activities will give you the opportunity to interact with other beginners (yes, most are beginners) and learn how to give your body the stimulation it needs without feeling like you have to overdo it. The instructors can also help you exercise correctly and prevent injury or overuse of your body. Consult a physician before you participate in any physical activities. Joining an intramural team may also help you find a social outlet. In Twentynine Palms, I encourage people to go rock climbing in Joshua Tree National Park. Perhaps adding a few more chores to your house list or starting a garden will give you the physical activity you need. A garden provides stimulation to your soul, a place to relax, and an opportunity to create. Gardening is the number one hobby in the United States, so there must be something about it for everyone, including those in high-rise apartments.

> A garden provides stimulation to your soul, a place to relax, and an opportunity to create.

If you got married and then your partner quickly deployed and you don't have any kids or anyone else living in your home, you might feel like it is a waste of time and food to cook. Not so . . . taking time to prepare healthy meals will stimulate your mind and give you the energizing food you need to avoid anxiety. Cooking is also a creative outlet when you create new foods and recreate your favorite recipes with new ingredients. Even better, invite over another at-home spouse and cook and eat together. If your body is not getting the nutrients it needs to stay healthy, you will develop anxiety and depression; more and more research is confirming the mind-body connection between the food we eat and our emotional state of being.

Prescriptive Medicine and Diets

Many people in depressed or anxious states want a magic pill, but prescription medication is often labeled for only short-term use. As a counselor, I recommend that clients get evaluated for prescriptive medications when they seem to be in a major crisis or if talk-oriented counseling isn't working. If you think about prescriptive medication, it really does seem like a miracle that with just a few specks of dust you can alter your entire mind-set. Now, if you can do that with a few specks of dust, imagine what you can do by eating a plate full of healthy food that contains many fresh specks of magic ingredients found in nonprocessed vegetables, grains, fruits, and meat. About 40 percent of modern medicine is derived from plants or synthesized to replicate plant material. Ultimately, your body is the one thing that is all yours and for which you alone are responsible; take care of it, do some research to decide what diet is best for you, and experiment with new foods and new ways of preparing the food to preserve the enzymes, vitamins, and minerals. Don't rely on supplements if you can help it; they are only supposed to be supplementary. If you are the deployed partner, you may be stuck with MREs (meals ready to eat)!

Send Your Love

Care packages are an excellent opportunity for both partners to exchange love over thousands of miles. Most deployments do not provide much opportunity for tourism, so the deployed partner probably won't be sending home too many tourist-type souvenirs, but he or she can send home love notes and self-made love cards or tokens of adoration. A nondeployed family member can send along some hard-to-find food to lighten everyone's mood. Magazines, books, and food are usually on the top on the list for deployed members. Photographs from home and letters are priceless. As a deployed member, if you can send letters and pictures from in-country, do so. Give yourself credit; when you write a letter to your family member, write down all the great things you are doing and how you are doing them. When you are struggling, write down what you are struggling with, what you are attempting to do about it, and the results. Remember, you don't have to be perfect.

Ditch Perfectionism

Trying to be perfect as our society defines it (e.g., always clean home, perfect kids, perfect body, perfect decorations, the best vacations, the best material goods, always saying the right things) will only cause you more anxiety that you don't need. Be happy with who you are, what you look like, and what you have. Where you are right now is right where you are supposed to be. There is no such thing as catching up on where you are supposed to be; there is only moving ahead to where you eventually want to be. Ditch the things that drag you down, and find things to lift you up, but once you make plans and are trying to do them as best you can, let yourself be satisfied with your efforts for that day. Your perfect day may end with your home being a wreck, your kids going to bed late, and you having accomplished nothing on your list of things to do; yet, you may have spent quality time with your family that was priceless. Comparing yourself to other wives, service members, or dependents can lead to either shame or pride, and neither one is constructive. As if on a teeter-totter, you may say, "Well, I'm doing better than she is" and feel great for a while, until you meet someone doing so much better than you on your superficial scale. Then you may say, "I'm so much worse than she is." Shame feels a lot like guilt, but it's more like a counterfeit of guilt. Guilt says you *made* a mistake; shame says you *are* a mistake. Guilt says you can make it better and should be constructive in correcting the problem; shame says hide it and get defensive so others don't ask or find out. Shame is a man-made version of guilt that can make us feel bad in a way that feels similar to guilt. Shame makes you feel like you are less than human, and pride makes you believe you are more than human. Neither one is true. You are just a human who makes mistakes and can correct them with time and effort in the right direction. You have strengths and weaknesses just like everyone else. Being sad and emotional is not a weakness; it can become your greatest strength. Emotional intelligence, a predictor of life success, measures how capable you are of identifying your emotions and actually *using* them positively to create positive outcomes in your relationships with others and within yourself.

> Ditch the things that drag you down and find things to lift you up.

Summary

Take care of yourself, take care of your children, and take care of your spouse, whether you are the deployed or nondeployed partner. Caring may be the key ingredient in successful, long-lasting relationships; it is the opposite of apathetically saying, "I don't care." With all the caring will come sadness and happiness and everything in between. Take your time deciding exactly what to do during the deployment—the one thing you have a lot of before your family member returns is time. Spend your time being creative, relaxing, and finding positive stimulation. Branch out to find good friends with whom you can be mutually supportive and participate in meaningful activities. Love yourself, love your life, and don't compare yourself to others. Paying attention to what you need to stay healthy and strong can be fulfilled in a number of different ways, but all of these ways should include being actively involved in good things that make you a better person so when you are reunited with your partner you will be better than ever. If you are deploying to another country with your active-duty service member, live it up!

Returning from Deployment: PTSD and Affairs

Returning from deployment should be a joyous occasion, but sometimes it is not. If you did not see combat and you were able to stay in touch with one another, then your family may resume business as usual. However, I have found that PTSD and affairs are frequent factors that need careful processing after a deployment. I focus on these two subjects because the skills needed to resolve them often overlap with other postdeployment problems.

There is a program currently on some military bases called FOCUS (Families OverComing Under Stress, http://focusproject. org/) that talks about deployment in terms of a spiral; no one enters or exits deployment the same. Children are born, friends and family die, and divorce happens. Thinking of a spiral as a three-dimensional shape rather than just a two-dimensional cycle, we can predict unpredictability. Your devoted partner may or may not cheat on you, your eleven-year-old may or may not hit puberty, and your partner might graduate from college; none of these things are predictable, so it's hard to adjust to them while halfway around the world. What about the service member? Will he or she be injured and have to leave early? Will he or she return with all of his or her limbs, hearing, eyesight, or mental functioning? You thought you knew your family, and they thought they knew you, but now you're not sure, and you couldn't prepare for everything. The feeling that follows is often helplessness or powerlessness. What used to work doesn't anymore. The old template for relating to your family members doesn't fit anymore. A new template has to be fashioned. When shoemakers or armor makers back in the day created their wares, if they were smart, they would take careful measurements. Then they would create a pattern or template with their new observations. After returning from deployment, take time to evaluate every interaction and situation with new eyes. Don't try to make things back to how they used to be: your little daughter grew up, your wife learned to live without you, your kids don't recognize you, the furniture was switched around, you can't find your old stuff, and new rules were made in your absence. Learning to adjust to change by assessing and adjusting yourself, *not others*, patiently is a principle that will work for you forever. No one is going to make the roller coaster any smaller, slower, or less steep to fit your fears.

Post-Traumatic Stress Disorder (PTSD)

This is the day you've waited upon for months; the deployment is over, and it will be great. Perhaps you have no desire to consider anything going wrong, but then, you've heard about PTSD, and you wonder if the recently deployed family member will have it. Deployed service members, you aren't the same person as you were before the deployment whether you have PTSD or not. You've changed in a year (plus or minus), just like you've changed dramatically every other year of your life. If you have kept your family members abreast of your daily or weekly experiences, you may feel like you've kept up on one another. If you've waited months (or had to wait months) in between, acclimating to one another may be more challenging.

While recently riding a plane from California to Virginia, I had the opportunity to spend several hours talking to the wife of a marine. She had been married almost ten years but had spent the minority of those years with her husband because of deployments and a TAD (temporary assignment of duty) that had already lasted three years! When her husband returned from the first deployment, she described him as "a zombie—he just played video games all the time and had no expression and wouldn't talk." Unfortunately, prescribed medication did not work on this service member, and the medication reportedly made things worse, so this good wife spent the next year carefully persuading her husband to talk to her about things. She asked him questions and listened carefully; she essentially acted like a full-time therapist. Each of the four successive deployments for this wife and husband relationship was not as bad, she said. They had learned their lesson.

> Ask questions and listen carefully.

This was the same woman I referred to in an earlier chapter who in later deployments had written in her journal every day and then sent the entire journal to her husband after three weeks of entries. By keeping him abreast of daily events, he seemed to better fit back into their family that now included several children. "I told him when I got my nails done, and he loved hearing about it. It takes dedication, but it's worth it," the wife related.

Relationships take investment, and if you aren't somehow invest-ing a little every day into the relationship, it starts to lose energy, she and I concluded.

Keep Talking

I liked how she kept at her husband until he got over his PTSD; she kept talking to him. You've probably heard people say, "I don't want to rehash it again" or "There's no use talking about it" or "I don't want to talk about it" or "It won't do any good and may make things worse" or any number of other excuses that people have to not talk about their traumatic experiences. The marine wife's husband tried these tactics with her, but she persisted, and fortunately, her husband did give way. Talking about traumatic experiences is hard. Most people cry and get angry and can hardly form the words to describe what they experienced. Some scream and have nightmares and can become angry and even violent. The good news is that every time you tell your traumatic story and allow emotions to enter in the story, it will be less distressing and you will gain more insight into the story. Prolonged Exposure (PE) therapy and Eye Movement Desensitization and Reprocess-ing (EMDR) are the most proven approaches to treating PTSD, but both give homework to clients to talk about their trauma and process details. The discussion and my suggestions below are derived from the principles of EMDR and PE but may not be in exact alignment with the theories. I use both of these therapeutic approaches frequently and have had much success in my attempts to foster recovery in service members.

It may be helpful to frame your combat and traumatic experi-ences as only part of the process of creating an artistic masterpiece out of yourself. Imagine pouring a melted substance into a mold to form a pot or some other work of art, then placing the mold and its contents into a hot kiln (oven) for a long time at high tempera-tures. When the mold and its contents are pulled out, they must be allowed to cool. When the art is pulled from the mold, after some cooling, it may not yet resemble art. A fine scalpel shaves off the excess material or whatever medium was poured in the mold. Paints and fillers and other things may need to be added before the artwork is complete. When a veteran returns from combat, he or she has been poured in a mold or something like that and has been through the kiln, and now it's his or her responsibility to put the finishing touches on himself or herself by going through counseling if necessary and facing his or her symptoms. The beautiful part of life is that you can choose how you want your art to appear, but if you lock yourself in a cabinet because you are fearful of judgment or further pain, you may miss the best changes yet to come.

Avoidance and Desensitization

One of the key criteria of PTSD that is often overlooked is avoidance. Avoidance of what? Anything that reminds them of the trauma. At first it might just be avoiding talking or thinking about it or walking away from other people who talk about it or remind them of it. Walking away lessens the distress. The only problem is that you never stop walking; you just keep on going because it follows you like a parasite. The only way to stop the parasite of haunting memories is to admit it's there and take appropriate measures to defeat it.

The "dirty secret" of PE therapy is that no matter how distressful the avoided activity might be, if you keep doing it, it will get better. Desensitization and reprocessing will occur. This is the same strategy behind EMDR (Eye Movement Desensitization and Reprocessing), which enables clients to work through scary thoughts and more fully adopt positive beliefs to replace disabling negative beliefs. After PE-trained therapists have done thorough assessment and established safety precautions with service members, they will give homework for veterans. Homework might include going to a crowded place for thirty to forty-five minutes until anxiety lessens and to do things that service members used to do before they had PTSD until the distress goes away. It's like jumping in a pool that at first feels uncomfortably cold, but the longer you play in it, the better it feels. Don't avoid the water. Jump in!

Reprocessing

You went swimming (metaphorically speaking) before your deployment. Do it again. Metaphorically, service members may say, "I'm not naïve anymore, and I know what can happen to someone who jumps in water; they could bump their head or drown or swallow water." Yes, that's true but not likely. Jumping in pools is an acceptable risk that you should take if you are physically capable of swimming.

Many good service members have returned home and decided that shopping is overrated. Some of them described how they would literally run in and out of the Exchange store only if they needed something badly and knew exactly where to find it. Some totally avoided crowded stores and scrutinized every individual therein and would not turn their backs to anyone. They preferred to have someone there that knew how to and could

> Live like you believe the positive affirmations until you really do believe them.

cover their backs. Others could only tolerate the anxiety of public places if they had a lucky rock to rub in their pockets or if they knew the area extremely well. None of the members affected by PTSD felt comfortable closing their eyes without someone watching for them. The fact is that you are physically capable of being an active member in society. You survived life for years before your deployment, and you can do it again. Be patient with yourself. Yes, a terrorist could be behind the grocery store aisle, but it isn't likely!

Returning to the metaphor of the work of art, as a returned service member, shaving off the extra material on yourself may include shedding the negative cognitions that make you fearful of people, places, and things. You will still be able to retain your amazing sensitivity to the world, but you won't have to live in fear anymore. You will be a more effective soldier, marine, airman, or sailor if you can realistically differentiate genuine, likely dangers (like drunk driving) from unlikely dangers (like the roof spontaneously falling on your head), because what we discover is that being on high arousal all the time actually lessens one's ability to differentiate big dangers from little dangers. Little things may seem huge, and huge things may seem small.

As a family, now that you're united, you should go do fun stuff together. Go out as often as possible to acclimate yourself to life in America again—Land of the Free. When you were in-country, you were forced to go out past the wire. Now that you're home, you need to force yourself to get out of the house and stay out until the stress and fear resolve naturally. You are capable of healing. You are capable of talking about the problem. You are capable of living a normal life. You are as safe as anyone, and desperate attempts to keep yourself safe (like living in a boarded-up house) may cause you to actually become less safe if they mean losing your job and family and resorting to negative coping skills (e.g., alcohol and drugs) to deal with the anxiety. Live like you believe the positive affirmations until you really do believe them. Believe that you are capable of recovering. Learn from your deployment experiences and let them be another step toward making yourself into an artistic masterpiece full of heightened compassion and caring.

Other PTSD Symptoms

Staying in your home and only leaving to go to work is no way to live. Getting angry and staying mad at friends and family is no way to live, and you could lose your family and friends if you keep avoiding them. Avoidance, however, is not the only symptom of

PTSD. The other symptoms include reexperiencing the original traumatic event and increased arousal. These symptoms could be indicated by trouble sleeping, difficulty concentrating, being constantly tense and on your guard, startling easily, decreased interest in activities, feeling detached, having restricted feelings, having flashbacks, having depression, being easily irritable, and more. What you do want to do is practice taking long (about four-second inhale and four-second exhale), slow, quiet breaths to keep yourself calm in anxiety-provoking situations. Breathing is one of the few things that universally, if done right, helps people deal with anxiety.

Even the worst panic attacks can be resolved with deliberate breathing. One man described how he overcame his fear of needles by deliberately breathing and paying attention to the sensations in his body when the nurse pulled out a needle. To his surprise, he didn't faint as he usually did, and the fear resolved itself. Service members who allow themselves to become acquainted with the fear and purposefully notice their rapid heart rates and the dread that overcomes them will find that it actually decreases and that they are still alive. The danger is when they become fearful of it happening again, because that fear ends up being the creator of the next episode. Let it happen. Do not fear it. The truth is that more traumatic experiences may occur in your life; you may never be free of them. However, you can overcome each of these traumatic memories and become stronger to survive the next one. Don't wake yourself up from your nightmares; they may be your body's primary means of processing the scary memory. My EMDR trainer suggested that the desensitizing bilateral stimulation in EMDR imitates the natural rapid eye movement (REM) that occurs when we dream.

Coping with Emotions

Almost everyone who tells a traumatic story is going to feel a lot of emotions—that is a good thing. I worry about the ones who don't show a lot of emotion, and I work to help them have those emotions. I worry about people who refuse to take responsibility for their emotions by blaming them on their spouses or others. Men will often cite how women are "overly emotional" as if it were a liability; however, they may be using this description even when the woman is just showing *some* emotion. Emotions are what allow us to process our experiences. You already do have emotions; however, you may not have much experience dealing with particular emotions, or you may not like that you are having certain emotions at all. Children experiencing a cut to their skin for the first time will howl and cry endlessly until they realize that it is only a bloody scratch. Adults experiencing new emotions in themselves (like the child's cut) may be fearful of what has happened to them and wonder if they will ever recover. However, rather than acknowledging the cut, they shamefully hide it and howl in silence. Denying a bodily function will not change that you are still having a bodily function. Emotions occur in our bodies and are natural movements used to signal us of something occurring. Why do people avoid talking about things in general? Because talking stirs up too many uncomfortable images and feelings that they don't want to go through right now or that they believe are signs of their weakness. Tragically, many well-intentioned officers or enlisted officers will suggest to their subordinates that they "suck it up," even when they really need medical attention. PTSD is not something you should "suck up." Yes, you will have to suck up the fear and do things you don't want to, but you shouldn't deny it, pretend it isn't happening, or avoid professional care.

Emotions are important biological sensations that humans have had for millennia, and emotions have helped humans survive and thrive through the most horrifying situations. Emotions are a part of your body, and getting to know an emotion better and what it is prompting you to do will help you get to know your body better and what your body needs to heal.

Peter Levine goes beyond EMDR and PE prescriptions to notice what your body is telling you through feelings, emotions, thoughts, and sensations and prescribes specific movements to work out emotions and unclog backed up pathways for the emotions to flow more smoothly. His therapeutic process, known as Somatic Experiencing (SE), was developed after he watched animals physically shake to shake off their traumatic captures by humans. He noticed that animals that failed to literally shake it off would die in the wild. Humans, he postulates, seem to have their own wild sides that facilitate shaking things out that they sometimes fail to acknowledge in processing their experiences. This approach may be worth some exploring for service members who are interested in learning more about how their bodies store and release traumatic memories.

Talk It Out or Write It Out, but Make It Visible

Growing up, I remember hearing about my dad's retired friend from Vietnam who refused to discuss what happened to him as a helicopter pilot. Thirty years later, as a retired, successful business owner with grandchildren and a reputation as a well-respected local religious leader, he still couldn't grapple with all the emotions of war. My father spoke about this man's trauma in hushed tones, as if it was sacred or something that shouldn't be talked about in public, if at all.

> When facing fears, start small and work your way up.

This seemed strange to me, even as a child, because I wondered how such a large man could still be scared of something that happened decades ago in a foreign country. He was probably just as perplexed. More than likely, he was fearful of crying in public and letting his emotions show.

My childhood perception was correct, and modern research and actual practices confirm it. I remember going to Kings Dominion in Virginia and adamantly refusing to ride any roller coaster. My parents pressured me to ride, but I refused. When I finally did get on, it was scarier than I thought it would be, but it was also a wonderful feeling to go up and down those hills. I started out small and then got bigger. This is a good strategy in facing fears: start small and work your way up. However, the dirty secret, as mentioned earlier, is that you can actually start big if you want, because all in all, the whole point is to become desensitized to it. Will you be a lot more scared on the bigger roller coaster? Of course. But if you keep getting on it, it's going to keep getting less scary—not more scary—because you'll realize that you are reasonably safe on it at some point.

What If There Was an Affair?

Returning from a deployment is usually a loving time for couples to foster love again, but sometimes it is the beginning of deep pain if an affair has occurred. If an affair happened during the deployment, then it will take months to fully recover; don't rush the process by demanding forgiveness or demanding a divorce. I recommend that couples don't decide whether to divorce or stay together until at least six months of counseling has been tried. Expect to fluctuate back and forth with wanting to stay and then wanting to go. That is normal.

An affair during deployment may be complicated by several things. The offending nondeploying spouse may have returned home and taken everything from the house and is not willing to work on anything. The offending spouse may be the active-duty member, and he or she may be unwilling to work on the relationship or even return to the home. All of these things are complicated when one considers that affairs are not even tolerated in the military, and solid evidence of an affair could cost the member his enlistment or commission. Fraternization (treating an enlisted service member as an equal) could also be enforced against the officer if the affair occurred between an officer and enlisted service member. Either way, the affair could cost the providing service member his or her main source of income for the family.

Another possible complicated scenario is if the extramarital involvement occurred between the nondeploying spouse and the deploying spouse's good friend who may be in the same military unit as the deploying spouse. I've seen this happen if the good friend had to stay back from deployment because of a personal issue. If the affair occurs between two active-duty deployed members, the whole unit may have to get involved. If the deployment is in a noncombat zone and the affair is with a local, the offending spouse may want to return to the affair after returning home or bring the paramour to the States. Sometimes the affair occurs while the spouse is deployed on a MEU (Marine Expeditionary Unit); in other words, they are on a navy boat and stop over at a local port where prostitutes can be easily found.

On the other hand, an affair may be something as simple as looking at pornography. Many a wife has mournfully explained how learning of her partner's pornography use feels just as painful as if a physical affair had occurred. To many people, this act constitutes an affair. Service members will readily acknowledge that pornography is easily accessible, even while on deployment, and that it is commonly used by lonely service members. The act of looking at pornography is often more of an anxiety reducer than what we typically think of as an affair, but to an offended spouse, it often feels the same. Viewing pornography does not mean that the offender is necessarily dissatisfied with his or her partner or that he or she even thinks the images are more attractive than his or her partner. However, the compulsive sexual behavior that Schneider defines as pornography dependence, compulsive masturbation, and voyeurism negatively affects the nonoffending partner's self-esteem and the overall marriage. In my observation, it can also have the effect of decreasing a partner's willingness to invest in the relationship and can negatively impact the quality of the marital relationship. Children are also often victims of their parents' sexual behavior and usually know something about what is happening.

Women may believe that their partners engaged in affairs because they were not attractive enough, but Hollywood news suggests that even the world's most beautiful people get cheated on. An affair is a choice that an individual makes. It is not caused by someone not being good enough, though that is a common excuse used to blame the other partner or justify further acts.

Recovering from an Affair

The marriage and family therapist William Doherty writes that affairs are common in our society, and many a good marriage has survived them. He points out three typical phases to recovery. Phase one, "Surge of Hope," includes telling one another that you are over it and really wanting to move on. This phase lasts about a month. Phase two, "No More Secrets," is much more intense and is identifiable when the injured partner starts asking for details about the affair and wanting clarification about why, when, and where. These questions should be answered and discussed honestly. Both partners should avoid self-righteousness postures, and the offending partner should answer the questions and tolerate ensuing anger and distrust while taking full responsibility for the infidelity. The process of recovery is full of ups and downs. This painful phase usually lasts for months, regardless of how small the infidelity may have been.

Phase three, "New Beginnings," is when the couple essentially starts over in their relationship. The excruciating pain and the terrible questions have subsided, healing has largely occurred, and the couple is ready to decide if the marriage is worth pursuing. Here the couple may start dating again and rebuilding a foundation of love. In this phase, couples will benefit from therapeutic trainings on conflict resolution, communication skills, and other marriage-enriching sessions. The energy of their relationship once drained by the affair will grow again.

An analogy that helps in understanding what must happen following an affair can be found in comparing the foundation of a relationship to the foundation of a house. This foundation is trust. An affair is like a catastrophic storm that damages the foundation as it rips the home from it and throws it upside down into the forest. Everything inside of the home is affected by the storm. Before the home can be rebuilt, the foundation must first be repaired. Sometimes the foundation has to be ripped out and a new one must be laid. Sometimes only parts of it will need repair. If you have ever watched a new home be built, you are familiar with how months are spent digging out the foundation, laying the rebar, and pouring the concrete. Then the next day you may see the entire frame of the house built. Building a foundation takes a long time; building the wooden frame of the house is easy and quick in comparison.

When the house is reconstructed on a solid foundation, everything that was in the old house must be evaluated for its suitability in the new home. Furniture may have been severely damaged and pictures on the wall may just need a new frame, but precious metals may be easily recovered. Rebuilding the family is equally time consuming after an affair; each part of the family life undergoes evaluation. Digging through the remnants of preaffair life may turn up delicate sentimental objects or memories that are colored, broken, and irreparable now. Even the most desensitized partner may be surprised and find himself or herself crying in deep sadness when a fond memory is recalled and examined in light of the affair.

Here are a few examples of how this might look following a deployment. A service member may look back on loving texts and letters from home and compare the dates to when his or her partner was engaging in extramarital relationships. Injured spouses will often recall how they enjoyed a loving memory in the arms of their partner only to recall how their loved one must have been thinking of another just the night before. Gifts given during the time of the affair may be especially poignant reminders of the painful betrayal. Missing money and missing time that could have been spent together will leave holes of despair that only time and space can heal.

Summary

The complexities of life may be even more complex following a deployment if the returning service member has PTSD or if an affair has occurred. Time is your best ally in these situations if it is accompanied by professional help and a willingness to do the right thing consistently. The emotional experiences that follow an affair or a traumatic event go deep and can leave permanent scars, despite healing. The body and mind can be greatly disturbed by traumatic experiences, but so can family relationships. Service members and their families will best serve one another following an affair if they are honest about their histories, symptoms, emotions, and fears. Every aspect of the family life may have to undergo close scrutiny before a full recovery is possible, and creating a new foundation of trust for the relationship is sometimes the best start. Paying close attention to the relationship and investing energy into one another after the deployment will help facilitate an environment where true healing can occur.

Use Your Heart

As the deploying family member, you are likely to have some experiences in your tour that are hair-raising, anger inducing, or devastatingly grief inducing. Most service members aren't prepared for what they actually see in combat. Sometimes the toughest looking are the least prepared. Preparing your heart to respond quickly and immediately to emotionally disturbing situations is good advice. Being able to identify what emotion you are having, decide if it's appropriate, and then transform it to use skills that are essential for surviving deployments. One marine shared with me how traumatic it was to be walking in a single-file line in a combat zone far from any visible enemies and then suddenly having the man in front of him fall to the ground from a sniper shot to the neck. A navy corpsman described the sickening scenes of mayhem that he witnessed each time he responded when an IED (improvised explosive device) would explode beneath a convoy of trucks and Humvees. Years later, these traumas continued to haunt these service members. These service members knew that such carnage could occur, but the surprise and the actual horror they experienced made their hearts sick. Some service members may be only minimally affected by these same scenes, while others experienced heart rate elevations years later from close calls with bombs even though no one was harmed. The difference between what severely impacts one service member's psyche and not another's is gradually becoming clearer for researchers and clinicians.

> Prepare your heart to respond quickly and immediately to emotionally disturbing situations.

How to Use Your Heart

Lt. Col. Grossman (Ret US Army) and Loren Christensen (Vietnam vet) are authors of the book *On Combat* and recommend that when something traumatic or adrenaline pumping happens to service members, they should not ignore their feelings. After the incident, they should not distract themselves by going back to their cots to watch movies and listen to their iPods; instead, they should sleep! Getting adequate quality sleep is essential to function at your highest. When a person is sleeping, his or her body naturally moves into a coherent state. Neurocardiologists believe that when the heart is coherent, it is in the ideal state for performing, healing, processing, and recovering. The word *coherence* implies order, structure, harmony, and alignment within and amongst systems—whether in atoms, organisms, social groups, planets, or galaxies." In humans, the "order, structure, harmony, and alignment" occurs between the mind, heart rhythms, nervous system, respiration, and every other part and system of the body.

Getting into a high coherent state prior to an expected military operation allows you to accumulate strength that can get you through rough spots by allowing you to think more clearly, make better decisions, and avoid emotional swings that drain energy and decrease your performance levels. One marine shared with me how he had been a machine gunner on top of a Humvee, an extremely dangerous place to be, during his deployment in Afghanistan and had been in firefights every time he left the base, which came out to dozens of times. His unit had suffered severe losses during the deployment, and many of his comrades did not return home. When he was checked by the doctor, there was no indication of physical problems, but his body had gotten stuck in a state of high anxiety. He had trouble sleeping, going out, and every other criterion for PTSD. He always had trouble relaxing. Like many service members stuck in high-anxiety states, his autonomic nervous system was not in coherence with the rest of his body. The autonomic nervous system, which controls 90 percent of your body's functions, regulates all involuntary functions, like elimination, digestion, sleep, endocrines or hormones, immunity, appetite, and breathing. This poor service member had problems with each of these areas and was lucky to get three to four hours of sleep. He was getting injured and sick more easily and losing his appetite daily.

By teaching this service member how to use his heart, he was able to process some of his traumatic experiences and calm himself in real time while finishing his service as an enlisted infantryman. His physical issues gradually improved over time, and he reported being able to concentrate better during everyday, normal work activities and to appreciate the stresses that those around him were also experiencing. He found that his relationships with his coworkers and commanders improved as he was able to regulate his emotions more purposefully and with greater focus. This service member was one of many that I helped to dissolve overwhelming anxieties and increase feelings of calm. In addition, I was able to help many military wives cope with the anxieties and depressions that came from being home and experiencing extreme loneliness while their husbands were deployed in a combat zone.

Applying HeartMath

In my own practice, I have found that HeartMath, a research-based approach to reducing anxiety and combat operations stress, is one of the most effective methods for helping people literally gain coherence in their lives. The techniques associated with Heart-Math have helped athletes perform at their highest levels, CEOs give their greatest presentations, and military families make their greatest recoveries. One wife described how she survived her marine husband's extensive three-year deployment using Heart-Math techniques that improved overall calm and sleep patterns for their whole family. She insisted that her husband also carry the emWave PSR (a HeartMath handheld biofeedback machine) everywhere he went while deployed, including patrols in the field. It went wherever he took his rifle.

HeartMath is a therapeutic approach that is being implemented by military counselors in military duty stations and in Veterans Affairs hospitals everywhere. The fastest way to coherence is using what HeartMath calls Quick Coherence. It is a three-step process. The following steps are quoted from the book *Transforming Stress*:

Step 1: Heart Focus

Focus your attention in the area of your heart. If this sounds confusing, try this: Focus on your right big toe and wiggle it. Now focus on your right elbow. Now gently focus in the center of your chest, the area of your heart. If you like, you can put your hand over your heart to help. If your mind wanders, just keep shifting your attention back to the area of your heart.

Step 2: Heart Breathing

As you focus on the area of your heart, imagine your breath is flowing in and out through that area. This helps your mind and energy to stay focused in the heart area and your respiration and heart rhythms to synchronize. Breathe slowly and gently in through your heart (to a count of five or six) and slowly and easily out through your heart (five or six count). Do this until your breathing feels smooth and balanced, not forced. You may discover that it's easier to find a slow and easy rhythm by counting "one thousand, two thousand." Breathe easily until you find a natural inner rhythm that feels good to you.

Step 3: Heart Feeling

Continue to breathe through the area of your heart. As you do so, recall a positive feeling, a time when you felt good inside, and try to re-experience it. This could be a feeling of appreciation or care toward a special person or a pet, a place you enjoy, or an activity that was fun. Allow yourself to feel this good feeling of appreciation or care. If you can't feel anything, it's OK. Just try to find a sincere attitude of appreciation or care. Once you've found a positive feeling or attitude, you can sustain it by continuing your Heart Focus, Heart Breathing, and Heart Feeling.

These are the steps that I used to help numerous service members overcome every type of family- and deployment-related issue. A recent pilot study conducted with service members diagnosed with PTSD found that using similar steps helped the participants to develop coherence, improve memory, and improve attention.

Daily practice using HeartMath has been self-reported by many military service members on the HeartMath Internet site to decrease anger and stress levels and increase relationship satisfaction. Practicing HeartMath Quick Coherence on a daily basis will create muscle memory in your heart that will allow you to quickly move into coherence on demand. The emWave, a HeartMath biofeedback device, allows for individuals to use it hands free while they are driving. You can know in the moment what your heart is doing and move yourself closer to a coherent state. This can prevent road rage or anxiety during combat operations and facilitate healing after combat.

The Heart: A Second Brain

A perusal of the HeartMath Internet site (HeartMath.org) and its many research findings confirms my own observations that the heart is critical to full-body recovery from any stressful situation, no matter how big or small. The heart is 60–65 percent neural cells, the same composition as the brain, which means the heart can store memory, process data, and make decisions. One could think of the brain and the heart as two separate computers in the body that can be used like two witnesses confirming that a decision is correct. The unique analysis of the heart is valuable in providing a different perspective and feeling than the brain can produce. In addition, when the brain has a metaphorical virus, the heart may have the metaphorical virus software to cure the virus. Neither organ can operate for long without the other.

Most people know that the heart is a muscle that pumps blood and that it miraculously can do this throughout your whole life without a vacation. What they don't know is that your heart also takes time to relax, at least, it will if you let it. Place your fingers on your neck or wrist and feel your pulse. Now take a long, slow breath in followed by a slow breath out. Repeat this until you notice the pattern of your heart. If you were not already extremely stressed out, you'll probably notice your heart rate speeds up when you breathe in and slows down when you breathe out. If you drew this out on a chart, it would look like a wave going up and down continually. The difference between the top of the wave and the lowest wave is called your heart rate variability (HRV). Neurocardiologists have found that yogis and those who practice deep meditation have the highest HRVs. The low points on the wave are when your heart takes a breather and relaxes. At the top of the wave is when your heart has rejuvenated and created energy for your body. A beautiful sine wave with gently rolling hills of high HRV is what you would see on a biofeedback's computer screen if you watched the most coherent of hearts beat over a few minutes.

Neural cells are found throughout your body and are the primary cells of the central nervous system. They receive data, process it, and aid in making decisions. Without them, you could not have muscle memory, which is when your muscles act somewhat independent of the brain. Interestingly, the memories of the heart are similar enough to the brain's memories that people who get heart transplants often have memories that aren't their own or crave cigarettes though they have never smoked.

The Heart as the Emotional Seat of the Body

Your heart seems to be the central command center (a brain) for your emotions; it is the emotional seat of the body. The heart's influence on the body's functioning is profound. Unknown to most, the heart is actually classified as a hormonal gland because it releases enormous amounts of hormones, especially the love hormone oxytocin that can weld strong attachments between people. That alone may explain why the heart is where people experience love. Anyone who has ever had his or her heart broken knows that it is a physically painful experience that actually hurts. This somatic experience suggests that it is not just a figment of your imagination that you are in grief. The patching and healing of the heart should be done similar to how you would rest a broken arm and give it time to heal without expecting it to recover immediately. Service members who have lost comrades in battle or almost lost their own lives will often experience massive doses of heartbreak and loss.

Your brain has no idea what is around it except for what our other organs (like the eyes) tell it. The ears send signals to the brain indicating a sound was heard, and the heart sends signals indicating emotional experience. Your brain decides what emotions it is experiencing largely depending on what messages the heart sends it. The heart sends these messages at least four different ways to the brain, according to HeartMath.org: "neurologically (through the transmission of nerve impulses), biochemically (via hormones and neurotransmitters), biophysically (through pressure waves), and energetically (through electromagnetic field interactions)."

Practicing HeartMath means paying attention to what your heart is detecting and trying to communicate. Listening to your heart's messages may allow you to identify the most positive things in your life and avoid the most negative ones, thus allowing you to make quick and healthy adjustments in your emotional strides forward. This could be compared to how you sidestep a telephone pole when your eyes detect it and alert your brain and muscles. The amygdala, a small structure at the bottom of your brain, is one of the receivers of your heart's electrical impulses. It actually changes its cell structure to synchronize with the heart's

Identify your own heart rhythms. Tune in to your heart.

electrical signals. Of course, emotions aren't just detected or felt with your heart and brain. They take place throughout your body. Have you ever asked yourself what an emotion is? Similar to how our eyes interpret reflected light to create images or our ears interpret sound waves, our emotions seem to be invisibly transferred, received, and interpreted. Theoretically, it seems like emotions are a combination of chemicals, electromagnetic waves, thoughts, feelings, and physical sensations all occurring simultaneously. Ignoring your emotions or becoming detached from them can cut you off from a significant part of what makes you human.

One soldier described on the HeartMath Internet site how his emotions were restored: "Just being able to feel again has probably been the most significant growth area that I have personally experienced. Most of us combat veterans have not even realized that we were disconnected and had literally lost feeling; it was 'just the way things were.' Personally, I feel as though I have spent the last forty years in an emotional fog that has just recently begun to lift, a little. I have really begun to feel music instead of just hearing or listening to it, along with sensing the pain others may be experiencing."

Many people say that you are what you think, or you are what you feel or do. I disagree; I have thousands of different thoughts, feelings, and actions every day. Which one am I? Also, what about when I feel hate and love at the same time? What am I if I want to kill and hug at the same time? Our souls often must comprehend a variety of conflicting messages all at the same time. We're proud of our spouses for serving honorably but are miserable for missing them. With so much happening inside of us, it's no wonder we sometimes feel crazy while our family members are deployed!

The heart and brain working together can masterfully sort this all out, but you have to be patient. The heart's stories may not be what you want to hear and may be conflicting with what your brain is telling you. Sometimes it is helpful to think of your heart as a large cauldron that you can let the emotions simmer in; the heart naturally softens them and makes them digestible. They can then be absorbed by the rest of your body and can actually energize and motivate you to do positive creative things. The heart is the place where most people feel things that they describe as spiritual. It is a good place to start when you are working in a relationship. Some of the sweetest memories and sensations are found in people's hearts. Small children will intuitively tune into their family members' hearts. They are sensitive to their parents' positive or negative emotions. The wonderful part of the HeartMath process is that you do not need to worry about changing anyone else. Simply identifying your own heart rhythms is adequate to make your world feel like a safer and happier place, regardless of the external stressors that may be around you. Tuning in to your own heart will also contribute to a greater sensitivity to other family members' heartaches or heart joys.

Applying Coherence

The character of Dan Millman in the movie *Peaceful Warrior* is based on a true person's experiences learning the hard way that feelings are not fact and that he is more than *just* emotions, thoughts, or actions. His intuitive trainer in the movie doggedly reminds him that there is more to life than just worrying about the past and future. Instead, he learns to live in the present and appreciate every moment. At the end of the movie, this present-centered thinking allows him to focus sufficiently to pull off a world-class gymnastic routine and eventually win a national title with his team despite shattering his femur ten months earlier. Coincidentally, I had a marine who was an Olympic hopeful in my office one day. After teaching him HeartMath Quick Coherence, he enthusiastically recognized it as a similar feeling to what he created in himself when meditating prior to performing his gymnastic routine in competitions. He applauded the idea of applying this preroutine focus to his everyday life, especially in his struggling marriage and family relationships. He realized that becoming more in touch with his heart prior to family interactions gave him a focus so he could avoid careless mistakes.

This service member recognized that he was more than just a brain, that every muscle in his body, including his heart, has muscle memory, and that with practice he would be able to create amazing relationships with family members. His brain and his heart became increasingly in sync with one another, and as he took time to listen to their messages and let them talk it out, he arrived at better conclusions. This syncing created what he described as a peace in his body and peace in his home.

Sadness Brings Coherence

I remember one time when I was at my desk at the end of a hectic day at work and I was trying to find coherence in myself, but my pulse was erratic and anxious. I was angry about some things, but when I thought on that, I only got worse. HeartMath teaches individuals to practice what is called Heart Feeling; you recall a positive memory of appreciation and care. This generally can slip you into coherence quickly and effortlessly. However, it wasn't working for me, so I decided to dig deeper and get in touch with my heart. I listened and found that I wanted to cry—my heart was sad, my soul was tired and weary. I wanted to know how the biofeedback machine would respond to sadness, so I set aside the anger and anxiety and promised to come back to them later. I focused on where the sadness was taking place and noticed that it felt like a hollowness inside of me. It felt gray and empty, and my heart seemed to be a small,

> ## Allow yourself to miss your family member and be sad, but that doesn't mean overwhelm him or her with your grief.

dark stone that sunk back and down into my chest. It was a scary feeling that I had to try really hard not to abandon. I told myself that I was safe and that this was for experimental purposes to understand myself better. The uncomfortable feeling intensified and I wondered if it really was going to be OK, but I stuck with it, listening to and feeling my heart. I kept the anger and anxiety at bay, trying to get just the most pure and raw feelings of sadness.

To my amazement, the biofeedback machine (i.e., emWave) showed a coherent display. It wasn't as high of coherence as with the positive feelings, but it was there. I decided to see how long it would last. I stayed with the feeling and tried to recall more sad experiences from my past because the sad feelings from before were dispersing. My heart seemed to be processing the sad feelings when I experienced them in their purity, and I couldn't hold them for more than about five minutes before they disappeared and were replaced by feelings of appreciation. With each sad memory I recalled, I was able to process it and end up with only appreciative feelings.

I would encourage anyone who is experiencing sad feelings at home or in-country to attempt to replicate my experience. Sadness is one of the few pure emotions that we can experience in our body. If you can separate "the clay ball" of sadness from "the clay ball" of anger and anxiety, you have a chance of experiencing a purifying emotion that can make you more appreciative of what you do have.

When I say allow yourself to miss your family member and be sad, I really mean that, but that doesn't mean overwhelming him or her with your grief. Don't contact his or her commander and demand that he or she come home because you feel so horrible. Instead, go talk to a professional counselor or a close friend and start the road to recovery. I have helped some terribly sad wives make it through intense loneliness by talking to them once or twice a week about their grief.

Summary

HeartMath is an excellent way to cope with hard feelings at any time, but it may be especially relevant for family members who are deployed or have a deployed family member. Even small children can be taught HeartMath and use it to increase their emotional awareness and performance. Practicing HeartMath will build heart strength and heart intelligence that will allow you to make it through difficult situations and help you to access more of the resources that your body has to offer. Our emotions start with the heart and then work their way throughout the body. If you are interested in processing your emotions better and becoming a more effective communicator and performer in whatever your duties are, practice the Quick Coherence technique daily before, during, and after your most difficult times.

Financial Issues

Few things can generate as much heat between a couple as money. Who gets to spend the money on what? How should the stay-at-home partner spend the money while the service member is deployed? What do you do with the extra money when you deploy? What vacations, gifts, hobbies, and other discretionary purchases are allowed? How much money should be saved, and how should it be saved?

I am not a financial counselor, and I encourage you to talk to one if you have technical questions about saving and spending money. What I will talk to you about is why money is regularly an issue when you join the military. You finally have a stable income, great insurance coverage, and your house and food are paid for or at least subsidized—no problems, right? Wrong. The military's attempts to create stability in its families are no match for credit cards and expensive vehicles. In the first decade of this

133

millennium, giant bonuses were offered to anyone who would sign up and stay in the military. I saw brand-new luxury vehicles, expensive sport cars, and large trucks driving all over the base I was on. Trips to the beach and expensive outings were permissible regularly when you had tens of thousands of dollars to spend. This precedent is no longer the case; my observations and client reports tell me that service members still buy expensive cars, but the cars often sit in their driveways because, after making the monthly payments, service members have no money for insurance and gas.

Money and Emotions

People attach their emotions to money, and they spend or don't spend it accordingly. You may think of money as security, or you may use it to satisfy your anxieties through retail therapy by making daily purchases that make you feel better. Family members either deployed or while at home waiting may use money to settle anxiety, generate entertainment, and in some way alter their moods. Addictions to alcohol, drugs, illicit sex, or gambling will sap a bank account dry before the next check comes

> Talk about a budget and talk about your beliefs regarding money.

in. Individual service members and married service members alike should identify how they are unconsciously spending their money and make more conscious decisions by understanding what emotions are driving their behaviors. Some may say that they have no emotions at all attached; they just spontaneously buy beer and live it up without thinking about it. This is just another way of satisfying a need for spontaneity; blowing money may be how they turn off their brains when their thoughts and emotions are overwhelming. Simply swiping a credit card or handing over cash may have some relief associated with it, like handing over one's attachments to all the problems in the world that money may represent.

Money is not just paper or numbers on your bank statement; it has an ability to link itself to people's emotions. There are several books written just for couples who are struggling with money issues. These books include *Til Debt Do Us Part* and *For Love or Money*. Money doesn't have to get in the way of your relationship succeeding; it can be an impetus for greater love and a means for creating lots of fond memories, security in a well-decorated home, or hope for the future when invested in a retirement fund. However, money in a marriage demands maturity. If one partner is unwilling to give up his or her childish irresponsibility and recklessly spends the money, resentment will build, followed by debt that will sink you to new lows.

A dependent wife once spent all of the money in her spouse's bank—tens of thousands of dollars—in less than a year, mostly on alcohol, while her husband was deployed. When he returned home, he was infuriated and unsure whether he could salvage the marriage. The wife insisted that she had been so depressed without him at home that she couldn't help spending it all. Unfortunately, this scenario is not that unusual. The only difference is that the money might disappear on some other nonessentials or unhealthy choices. In this case, there was an anxiety-reducing emotion attached to the money; the act of spending the money was almost as mood altering as the alcohol she purchased. Spending the money represented a way to forget about her loneliness, alleviate problems, and have a good time while her husband was deployed.

If money is a means of security for you, you may be able to save and accumulate money well. This is generally a good association as long as it does not lead to double standards (you can spend the money but others cannot). A common complaint I hear is that the wage earner buys himself or herself a new truck, but the spouse has to scrape by with worn-out shoes and no vehicle at all. If money makes you nervous and you get anxious just talking about it, it's time to grow up.

Money and Communication

One woman shared how she didn't even want to talk to her husband about money, and she wanted him to tell her what to buy. This may be a dream for some men, but in this case it kept her from contributing to family decisions and fully participating in the relationship. After a few sessions of counseling, she proudly announced that she and her husband had some deep discussions, and now she understood why they so rarely had extra spending money and where the money was going. She could stop resenting her husband and start enjoying the responsibility of making healthy choices with her life partner.

Talk about a budget and talk about your beliefs regarding money. Find out what your spouse's beliefs are with regard to how money should be spent, negotiate your differences, and discuss third options that may be more balanced views than either of yours alone. If your beliefs about money differ, don't be surprised. That's a good thing. An old saying in business credited to William Wrigley Jr. is, "If two partners always agree, then one of them is not necessary." The differences allow for new approaches to problem resolution.

Your partner's perspectives and uses for money may broaden your ability to appreciate money's uses. I have heard people from both wealthy and poor families say that money is no substance and that they like living it up and spending the money while they have it. I've likewise heard people from poor and wealthy families tell me that money should be accumulated and carefully spent. Express confidence in one another and avoid condescension towards one another about perspectives on money or one's history of spending it. Don't use your socioeconomic or familial background to justify reckless and irresponsible actions or conversely use your partner's bad decisions to justify double standards for who can or cannot spend money or make financial decisions.

Too often, partners don't communicate at all about spending money. I was surprised to learn that many military wives have no access to the bank account, no credit or debit cards in their names, and no spending power at all. These same individuals may not even know how much money their partners make or how the money is spent. I have only seen this with the wife, but it may be possible with dependent husbands as well. Spouses may feel awkward asking their partners, who work so hard, to divulge how much money they make or tell them how to spend it. Working spouses may even act in ways that send the message, "This is my money. Be grateful if I give you any." I have actually heard this message verbalized many times by service members, and it is said directly and unequivocally because they believe it.

A balanced relationship will include a balance of power and extensive discussion about any large financial decisions until both partners agree. Returning to the idea of your mind and heart working coherently, the same analogy could be used for a husband and wife working coherently to balance the budget. The heart may be the better of the two communicators (there are actually more nerves running from the heart to the brain), and the brain may have different ways of processing things, but no good decision will be made without confirmation from both the brain and the heart. Financial decisions that are made in a family with both the husband's and wife's approval are generally more healthy for the relationship than unilateral decisions.

Money, Trust, and Control

The person who earns the money may feel entitled to use the money however he or she pleases, regardless of the other family members' needs. Sometimes this means that kids suffer and other times only a marital partner. I asked some of these service members what made them so possessive that they were unwilling to share their money even in the most intimate of human relationships. They reasoned that they had learned it while in boot camp, and in training they were taught that they are to look out for their own gear and guard expensive SAPI (Small Arms Protective

Insert) plates and other easy-to-lose equipment. They alone were responsible for it, and they were not to let anyone take it.

I believe this may have genuinely contributed to their thinking, but I think it was a poor excuse overall. Their possessive reasoning justified acts of entitlement that detracted from what could have been much healthier families. One friend of mine described how his girlfriend's father returned from deployment and began reminding his daughter regularly that the car she drove was his, not hers, and he even pulled out the title and insurance paperwork and pointed to his name on the documents to emphasize the point. The father's possessive behavior only served to make his daughter more fearful of him and less likely to share her thoughts and feelings with him in the future. The daughter's family wondered if the father's new jealous possessiveness, which was being expressed in other ways as well, was related to PTSD, but since he had no diagnosis of such, they could only assume that his recent deployment served as an excuse to act more possessively. This sounds strange, but if one's peers have been acting possessively or disrespectfully on a deployment and selfishness is the norm and group climate, it is easy to return home and continue in this mind-set.

Service members may also abuse their spouses' trust when they suggest that stay-at-home spouses should trust them completely and unquestioningly on money issues and that said spouses do not need access to any accounts or expenditure lists. It is my interpretation that the founding fathers of this country created the government with a trust in other people but believed that everyone has weaknesses and that power and money can corrupt one's original good intentions. Thus, they created checks and balances. Trust should also be the foundation of your family relationships, but sometimes you may have to put yourself or a partner in check. A service member who declares himself or herself the omnipotent protector of the money is not unlike an elected leader who usurps power from the very people who elected him or her.

Recovering from Reckless Spending

If you returned from deployment and your money was all gone because of a partner's reckless spending, you may feel devastated, angry, and betrayed. You expected to have thousands in the bank (because you get paid extra on deployment), but it is all gone, and maybe you are even in debt now. It is not amusing and it may be the final nail in the coffin of an already deceased marriage, especially if it was coupled with infidelity and other indicators of irresponsibility and emotional immaturity. However, one man shared with me that he did not want to tell his children when he got older that he divorced their mother because she bought a new car while he was gone. He was able to overlook what he saw as an irresponsible and inappropriate unilateral decision and focus on the future; he saw what could be a happy future with nurturance. Together, he and his wife diligently worked on every aspect of their marriage in counseling and made their weaknesses into strengths. Marriages are much like living organisms in that if they are left unnurtured or overlooked, they will die. As a marriage and family therapist, I make it my business to help individuals learn to nurture their marriages and families back to life.

Recovering from the breach in trust that follows poor financial decisions is difficult. Both persons are hurt and struggling and may not even know what contributed to the problem. It is as if you and your partner have gone into combat and been shot, perhaps because one or both of you made poor choices or were negligent, causing both of you to be gunned down. Separated from your unit, you and your spouse are two injured soldiers trying to limp back to safety, heavily leaning on one another. Sometimes it is just too much and you collapse, but if you can make it to a doctor or medic, he or she can help bind up your injuries and provide casts and supports for you to heal internally. Emotionally, you and your partner may both be severely injured from bad decisions and feel like you are stuck in the desert with no hope. Limp to a counselor and get some support so you can start the healing process for emotional injuries and forgive debts. Think of counseling as building a cast to assist in healing and to eventually lead to a full recovery. Following an hour-long first session, I regularly tell clients not to do anything to try and change the relationship. Instead, I beg them to rest, heal, and enjoy spending time together without trying to fix anything. To try and fix the relationship with just one hour of counseling would be like trying to stand up on a broken leg when the cast hasn't even set yet.

Collaborating on Money

If both spouses are aware of the expenses and income and have decision-making power, it becomes more likely that both partners' needs will be met and that no single person will have more say than another. Sharing financial decision-making opportunities between partners facilitates both parties learning how to be responsible with money and accountable for their expenditures. Money just happens to be one of the weapons that can be used to emotionally injure a spouse if teamwork is not a prevailing theme. Viewing your partner as a true partner and not an enemy is a start in defeating the battle against emotional spending. A good start might also be creating a budget, discussing every expense together, and creating both short- and long-term financial goals. You wouldn't want to go into battle without a plan, plenty of practice, and a clear mission goal. Think of every financial decision as a chance to practice your financial response plan and prepare for unforeseen financial attacks from outside of your family. Invest time in educating yourself and your partner about finances. Recognize that each of you will make mistakes in spending sometimes. Spend time with one another discussing the mistakes without pointing fingers and blaming one another for whatever your situation currently might be. Instead, admit that where you are is where you are, and it is not because you are behind or because you failed. You can always bounce back; it just might take years of hard work. That hard work will pay off, and what once was a weakness could become a strength that allows you to have more insight than the average couple on what contributes to financial debt and problems. Ideally in a committed relationship in which partners can trust one another, the money can be consecrated between the two of them to create a safe, happy family. You must make yourself one hundred percent accountable to your family for how you spend your money. A good question to ask yourself is whether you are putting your own emotional needs and spending cravings in front of your family's needs. Plenty of good parents I know have quit expensive hobbies so they could spend more time and money investing in their children, and they have no regrets.

Preventatives

If you are worried about your spouse spending all the money while you are deployed or if you are worried that you will spend all the money, you can set up allotments that go to a separate account so there is enough money to cover groceries, gas, and incidentals. You can also create a joint account and have a portion of the money go to a savings account, since you'll be making a little extra during the deployment. Set up automatic payments through your bank's bill pay system or have the money drafted straight out of your account each month. Cut up your credit cards and avoid debt like the plague. Pay in cash only if you don't want to balance a checkbook. Pay the bills first. Read books with specific advice for getting out of debt. Stay away from shady fast-money and debt-elimination programs. Live within your means.

Family Equity and Trust

Equity is a little different from the word equality, because equity acknowledges that dividing quantities of resources equally between persons may be inadequate or too much, depending on the receiver. A child would not be expected to work the same amount as an adult. A woman would not be expected to go without her feminine products because the man didn't need to buy them. In our everyday life, we act in ways that create equity. When we consciously make choices to create equity, we are acting on a principle that will create harmony. My younger brother was more physically active than me, and he wore out his clothes faster than me. Sometimes it was necessary for my mother to buy him a new jacket or pair of shoes before I got a new pair. I thought nothing of it and took pride in my ability to make clothes last, but my mother taught me a lesson one day to prevent me from ever becoming jealous of my brother: "I will buy you things when you need them, but for now your brother's needs are greater than yours." Later on, I'm sure my needs balanced out the spending that my mother invested in us, but if I had been so focused on the

> You still own what is yours, but you must now skillfully and carefully distribute your resources with at least one other person.

present that I missed the timetable, I would have become bitter and inharmonious in my relationship with both my mother and siblings. Perhaps life is unfair, or perhaps it is incredibly fair, and myopic perspectives cannot appreciate the just way that fairness is dealt out over a lifetime.

When you sign up to be in a family, you are signing up to sacrifice. You still own what is yours, but you must now skillfully and carefully distribute your resources with at least one other person. At times, your needs will require larger amounts of money, and at other times, your partner's needs will require large sums of money. Making the money available to one another is an important way of showing trust. If you can't trust your partner yet because of a history of bad choices, keep loving him or her. Hopefully, he or she will earn back the trust with time by doing the right thing consistently. An example of how trust and love are different can be found in the following analogy: If my son is stealing money from me, I am not likely to leave money lying around the home.

It may be possible that your partner genuinely is not capable of responsibly handling money. This can be gauged based on a history of unpaid debt, late fees, reckless spending, expensive addictions, or even bankruptcy. In such cases, the partners should work together to create a plan that both partners can agree to. This plan may include knocking out debts using a specific approach: setting bills to be paid on time using an auto pay. An even more restrictive agreement might be that only a percentage of the money is made available to the spouse. Perhaps the active-duty spouse agrees that his or her partner only gets enough money to spend for lunch and a few incidentals each week. This practice should be followed until both partners agree that the restricted spouse has worked through whatever emotional beliefs were preventing him or her from spending responsibly. While the service member is deployed, though, it is in the best interest of the stateside partner to not create debt. Serious debt can impact a service member's work, and bill payers will call commands seeking payment. During a deployment, such calls and stress could cause the service member to become anxious about how the money is being spent and thus distract him or her from his or her mission in-country. Such a distraction could put a lot of people's lives in danger when people are depending on the service member to be completely focused in a combat or life-saving situation. Placing severe restrictions on yourself or your partner should be temporary, a last resort, and something that you both agree is necessary.

Professional Help

Personal counseling and marital counseling sometimes can help individuals work through their emotional issues enough that they lose their insecurities and are then ready to face the responsibilities of money. Seek out professional financial advisors, read books on money, and ask nonbiased professional sources for help on deciding how best to be stewards of your money. My recommendation is that you spend some of your money to take your sweetheart on dates and create memorable vacations that aren't too heavy on the pocketbook. The average divorce is $15,000; it is much cheaper to invest in your relationship and become an expert on money than to pay for a divorce attorney. Remember how much you spent on your partner when you were just dating? Set aside some money to keep your family together, because your family may be the one thing

Set aside some money to keep your family together.

you have to show for your life in the end. If your partner had a serious physical illness like cancer, how much would you spend on his or her recovery? Most people will go bankrupt to save their partners, yet they may struggle with losing a few thousand dollars because of some poor mentally or emotionally irresponsible decisions that, with time, could be worked through. If you are learning from your poor decisions and making increasingly responsible decisions, press forward and look back only to learn from your mistakes.

Summary

Spend your money with a perspective that includes your spouse as a full partner and his or her needs. Plan together and discuss regularly where the money is going. Prepare months before the deployment and know how the money will be saved or budgeted. Be honest about your level of competency with spending money and seek professional help if you are incompetent. Our use of money is clearly tied to our emotions. If we are irresponsible with our emotions, we will be irresponsible with our money. Trust and love are closely tied to one another, and one's use of another's money is an indicator of how strong the love and trust really is. If you don't like talking about money, do it anyway! You'll save yourself a lot of heartache if you can learn to recognize your unavoidable ties to money and use your resources to bless your family rather than satisfy your own lusts.

Addictions

Whether it's gambling, alcohol, pornography, or shopping, an addiction is an addiction. Most of us live happy lives that include ups and downs, and the ups and downs balance out in the end. Imagine a line representing the median. A mood-altering substance or activity can make it so that I hardly ever notice the lows anymore, but over time I get so I need the substance or activity just to get back up to the median at all, and I might never get up above it like I used to, even with the mood-altering addiction.

An Addict Mind-Set

A service member reported that he didn't think he really had a gambling problem. He blew his reenlistment money, maxed out all his credit cards, borrowed from friends, and got other loans that he gambled away. This poor fellow said he started almost a decade ago, but it was just a few bucks on the table; then it became a few hundred, and then he won big! He believed that he could win big again. He was smart, and he knew everything was stacked in the dealer's favor, but he told himself that since he had done it once, he would win again. He told himself he just needed one more big win to be satisfied for a while. Now he had trouble sleeping at night because he was in so much debt; he had lost the trust of his friends, his command, and his family. He explained that he was actually less interested in the money and that it was worthless to him. What he loved was the excitement of winning!

Yet, he couldn't admit that he even had a problem. He still believed that he was in control of his behavior. Most of the time, people who have an addiction will minimize their behavior and say something like, "Well I'm not as bad as [somebody else]." Then they will identify how the other person uses a different substance, uses a substance more often,

> Be proactive in avoiding anything that could possibly become an addiction.

uses a substance in a larger degree, uses a substance with more intensity, or uses a substance in a different way than they do. The alcoholic thinks the marijuana user is worse, the marijuana user thinks the cocaine addict is worse, the cocaine addict thinks the heroin addict is worse, the heroin addict thinks somebody else does it more than him or her, and so on. I spoke to many service members who had a history of serious drug addiction but were currently sober. They struggled with identifying new coping skills to replace their former addictions. They went to treatment, but in my experience, anyone in the military who confessed to using drugs or failed a urinalysis for drugs other than what he or she was prescribed by a physician or a psychiatrist was quickly separated from the military. Be proactive in avoiding anything that could possibly become an addition.

Addiction and Emotions

Retail therapy is a name for a shopping addiction. It is a form of addiction that is similar to gambling; there are bright lights and appealing colors, and shopping can be done with friends and a credit card anywhere, including your own home. Military family members may be tempted to use their stable incomes to justify excessive shopping because they can "always pay it back later," they tell themselves. Again, all of us associate emotions with money, and when we start shopping all the time, we are probably compensating for an emotional issue somehow. Most likely there is a deficit in healthy coping skills to deal with strong emotions. The gambler in the story above described how he sat in a chair facing the dealer. He said that while he was gambling, he knew that he should leave. He knew that he should have walked around for a while and stopped, but he didn't. The urge to stay and play was irresistible. He described how he felt as if he were beside himself, watching himself do something that he knew was wrong but was powerless to stop. Swiping the credit card one more time is just as much of an emotional rush or release of emotion. These addictions are problematic because they become the catchall means of coping with pent-up and unwanted emotions.

Unhealthy mood-altering activities and mood-altering substances have a lot in common and are used to deal with unwanted emotions. There are positive mood-altering activities that should be used regularly, but if an activity is taking a toll on your relationships with family and friends, you need to change it. Addictions don't usually happen all at once. Like a slippery slope, there are years of gradual, almost imperceptible, changes, followed by a sudden, unstoppable drop downward. It took almost a decade for the gambler to finally start winning big, and then he started wagering bigger and bigger—until he lost it all and fell off the slippery slope's cliff. Once he was off the precipice, he no longer cared whose trust he lost or who he had to beg or borrow from to get money; he was only interested in winning one more time, and then he'd be okay. He was embarrassed and laughed when talking about his gigantic debt, but he felt a sense of guilt and a lot of shame. The shame kept him going in his bad habit. The more shame he felt, the more he needed something to alter his mood — like gambling.

The gambler tried to blame his depression on the cards and the bad runs, but his time was up. He'd used up his good luck. He had gone from a rational, frugal, sober-minded, selfless, sacrificing service member to a reckless gambler who ended up losing his security clearance in the military because his command no longer trusted him. His career was in jeopardy, and his relationships with peers, friends, and family were all in danger. I would compare it to when you're outside and you can tell that it's getting dark, but you continue to play outside. You can see the house in the distance lit up brightly, but you continue to play until you are running with friends and then run into a tree that you didn't see because the darkness had crept in so completely. In contrast, the person who notices it is getting dark and goes in the house will turn around almost instantly and see how dark it really is outside as his or her eyes adjust to the light inside. If your friends start telling you that they're going home because it's too dark, listen to them and get help finding your way back out. The gambler will eventually find his way back out of debt, but he will never lose his desire for gambling with high stakes. If he returns to the tables again, he'll be betting thousands all over again within a couple hours. He'll never get the same satisfaction from penny machines, just like an alcoholic won't get much buzz from a wine cooler, no matter how long he or she has been sober.

> **If an activity is taking a toll on your relationships with family and friends, you need to change it.**

Service members or their family members may name many reasons why they are addicted, including long hours, chronic pain from injuries in the service, bad command relationships, grief over the loss of a friend, trauma from deployment, or problems at home. All of these things could be contributing to the addiction or could be why they turned to the mood-altering activities in the first place. These problems will only be compounded by an addiction, despite temporary relief from unwanted emotions.

Summary

Fortunately for service members, they have lots of resources at their duty stations to help them with addictions and financial issues, and often commands are willing to help them budget their money and monitor them. Addictions are real and should not be ignored or downplayed, nor kept secret; such behavior will only further the shame and compound the problems on all family members, regardless of whether it is the service member or partner that is addicted. Addictions are often tied to our emotional state of being, and if you think there is a problem, you should seek out a thorough professional evaluation (e.g., MilitaryOneSource. com) conducted by a licensed counselor to identify and process root sources of addictive behaviors and help family members identify new means of coping with military life's difficulties.

Alcoholism and Codependence in Military Families

We all know drinking and drugging is a big problem at colleges, but it is also a significant problem in the military, despite the fact that most active-duty service members begin their careers under the legal drinking age. If you aren't already drinking alcohol, don't start. You never know whether you are a potential alcoholic until it is too late. I am not a drug and alcohol counselor and am not going to go over the steps to quit, but I will discuss alcoholism's effects on families in the military. I should mention that alcoholism often has parallels to other unhealthy family patterns, so this chapter's principles may be applicable to your family even if alcohol itself is not the problem.

An alcohol and drug counselor on base that I interviewed emphasized to me that alcohol treatment is available to service members and is not a punitive process; this counselor stated that even "good" marines sometimes have severe problems. Military balls, wet downs, and warrior's nights have culturally become times for service members to drink heavily. This counselor and I regularly saw service members after these events because each had some kind of serious alcohol-related incident occur, from public drunkenness to a DUI to domestic violence. The Afghanistan and Iraq operations are the longest military actions in US history since Vietnam, and they have taken a huge toll on service members; these operations have resulted in significant mental health issues, increased alcohol and prescription drug use, suicide increases, and domestic violence increases in the military.

If you even think someone may have a problem with alcohol, just ask him or her these four questions. If they say "yes" to any of them, they should get help.

1. Have you ever felt you should *cut* down on your drinking?
2. Have people *annoyed* you by criticizing your drinking?
3. Have you ever felt bad or *guilty* about your drinking?
4. Have you ever had a drink first thing in the morning to steady your nerves or get rid of a hangover (*eye*-opener)?

These questions are the CAGE questions (see italicized words). They are utilized by professionals on military bases to identify alcoholism. Every unit in the military has a substance abuse officer who works with anyone who has an alcohol-related incident or an alcohol problem. The base has professional counselors who do a more thorough evaluation of chemical dependence, and they can refer the service member to groups or a residential treatment center. Rarely do service members volunteer for this help from my experience, and they often share with counselors what great lengths they have gone through to conceal

If you aren't already drinking alcohol, don't start.

their alcohol dependence. The amount of alcohol that service members told me they drink was often staggering to even hear, yet many of them would say that they didn't think it was that much when compared to their friends. Usually, an alcoholic does not even recognize that his or her behaviors qualify him or her as an alcoholic, and alcoholics are rarely self-motivated to seek out change. More often than not, service members will only show up for chemical dependence treatment after some third party has gotten involved or they have hit rock bottom in some important part of their lives, like in their family relationships. Following a deployment, service members are much more likely to start using alcohol heavily, more often, and with more associated problems, and this alcohol abuse could be tied to PTSD from combat-related experiences. For this reason, a professional should be sought to rule this out as a contributing factor and the alcoholic should get counseling-specific help related to this disorder.

Families and Codependence

If you are a spouse of a service member that drinks too much, you are probably thinking that you don't want to ruin your partner's career by referring your partner to counseling, exposing his or her abuse in the home, or telling people about his or her substance abuse. The truth is that yes, his or her career could be ruined, but it's not because you pointed it out; it's because of his or her bad decisions or failure to get help earlier. In my experience, it was rare for a service member to get in any trouble for seeking help for his or her alcoholism if he or she sought it before getting in legal trouble. More often than not, it would actually earn the respect of peers, and at worst, the command saw it as more of an annoyance that took away time from work.

If your family member is abusing alcohol, he or she is going to crash in some or all dimensions of his or her life eventually. Hopefully you can capitalize on the small crashes in the beginning to help motivate him or her to get help early. If you cover up the small crashes, the family member will start to believe he or she can get away with more and more. By encouraging him or her to get help, you may prevent a more serious crash in which someone is seriously hurt later on. If getting help is postponed, a lot more than the service member's career could be ruined. Protecting your family member from consequences often only leads to greater indiscretions, more entitlement, more secrecy, and more permanent injury.

Let's compare alcohol's damage to a physical cut or a sickness. Any serious cut or injury deserves a trip to the emergency room to get X-rays, set bones, and apply sutures. Living with alcoholism and not seeking help is like ignoring a cut or injury that festers and leads to fever and more serious problems. Too often the family

> Be a hero by getting professional help and encouraging your family member or friend to participate completely.

members don't necessarily ignore the problem but try to cure the problem themselves or cover it up to avoid attention because of how they fear it will reflect on them.

Trying to solve the alcoholism problem yourself, once its infection has set in, is not going to work; you need the counseling equivalent of antibiotics and professional attention. When a family member is an alcoholic, he or she is sick, and if he or she has a spouse or close family member attending to his or her needs in secrecy, then usually that family member gets sick too. You may say, "I'm not sick—only the alcoholic is!" Let me demonstrate my point in the following illustration and stories that follow.

Picture yourself as a stick figure inside of a circle. The circle represents your boundaries and your dominion. This is you as an independent individual. Imagine your partner inside a similar but separate circle on the paper.

Two independent individuals living happily satisfied lives. What happens to those circles when the persons get married? Most say that you should abolish the individual circles and combine into one big circle that encapsulates both stick figures.

Nope. That's how babies and their parents exist: in a state of total dependence. Parents change their babies' clothes and diapers, feed them, and bathe them. If you drew just one big circle around the stick figures and abolished their individual circles, then who's responsible for taking care of you? Would the nonactive-duty spouse be responsible for going into work for the service member if he or she were sick or didn't get up on time? Is he or she responsible for waking his or her spouse up for work? When you're an alcoholic, it actually does get that confusing: codependent family members end up making a lot of excuses for their hungover service members. They end up doing their online college courses for them or making excuses for them when they say rude things in social settings or cleaning up their vomit and bathing them before tucking them into bed. What's wrong with all that, you say? Everything, but it isn't always obvious.

It is the beginning and the end of an insidious pattern that leaves the alcoholic doing about as much as the dependent baby and the sober partner acting like Momma. Codependence is, in my illustration, drawn a little differently than dependence is. It would be drawn with an overlap between the two independent circles, with a large shaded area between them where they overlap.

Codependence is different from simply being dependent because it refers to an unhealthy symbiotic relationship between two persons who only appear to be acting independently in their emotional relationship. The alcoholic and his or her enabling family member start to act almost like a parasite and host relationship in which both persons are not being honest about the problems that are occurring. They want the relationship to work and are willing to overlook serious problems simply to maintain the relationship and meet their own emotional needs rather than do what would really help each other over the long run.

Alcoholics and their enabling family members both may have poor insight into the dynamics of codependence occurring in their families. Sometimes the service member is the alcoholic and sometimes another family member is the alcoholic; either way, it will eventually hurt the family and the service member's ability to give his or her best in the service. If you are the nonalcoholic, you may have tried to save your partner by jumping in to save him or her from drowning, and you ended up almost drowning when the alcoholic clung to you like a life preserver. This is not because the alcoholic doesn't like you; it is only because, at the time, it seemed like the best idea, and you made yourself appear to be a solid buoy. Perhaps you overestimated your foundation in the shifting water and thought you could actually support the flailing family member by yourself. In teaching lifeguards how to save a drowning person, the advice is to not get in the water with the drowning person because there is a much higher chance that you both will drown. Instead, lifeguards at pools are advised to stay on the shore and reach with a limb or pole or throw a buoy. Only in extreme cases should lifeguards sneak up behind the drowning person and with one arm pull him or her out of the pool, and that is only with lots of instruction, training, and practice.

Codependent, nonalcoholic partners might have told themselves any number of rational things that led them to becoming enablers and jumping in the water to rescue the family member, resulting in them essentially overfunctioning as family members. It is human nature to want to help those you care about and to wear yourself out trying to do it or to jump into the water and try to force your alcoholic family member out rather than extending a hand from the shore. Maybe you even feel sorry for your partner and believe that it is your role to rescue him or her and point him or her to help. More than likely, the alcoholic partner already knows that he or she is in deep water and that he or she should get help. Don't be a hero by jumping in. Be a hero instead by getting professional help (e.g., MilitaryOneSource.com) and encouraging your family member to participate completely. Unfortunately, sometimes family members will get professional help and then wish they hadn't sought the help because things get harder after the professionals get involved. However, over the long run, these same individuals are usually grateful, and looking back, they can see that the path was hard but worth it.

Family members may feel a need to overfunction to help the service member be successful but may actually wear themselves out in the process and lose perspective of their own needs. They may desperately want their military service member to get a promotion or not get in trouble and get positive attention. It may be necessary to do more than the average family member in a civilian family to help a service member, but there need to be limits and boundaries. The goal should be for each person to recognize what his or her personal responsibilities are and to carry them out independently. An example is if a service member doesn't get a promotion, he or she can't blame his or her parents or spouse but must accept that it was his or her responsibility alone. If a family member or service member believes he or she cannot carry out these responsibilities independently, then it may be necessary to determine which responsibilities are most important and focus on those and cut back on extraneous time wasters, like drinking alcohol, playing video games, or watching the latest reality show. Social time is important, but if it is causing your family relationships to fail, it should be abbreviated. If the alcoholic family member refuses to do his or her responsibilities and insists that they are not his or hers to fulfill, then, to use a sports analogy, the team will fail for a game or two. However, losing one or two games is better than losing the team if both partners ignore the debilitating problems and have to disband. In a combat setting, any one person who fails to fulfill his or her post (independent responsibilities) could cost everyone their lives. In a family, it could cost you those most dear to you.

A team might lose its coherence and lose team players if one player is overfunctioning by trying to play the positions of goalie, offense, and defense while the other team players do whatever they want on or off the field. The overfunctioning team player says that it is necessary to win, but ultimately he or she will actually be blamed for losing the game. An example of this in real life is when an overfunctioning family member tries desperately to give direction and help to an alcoholic but ultimately is labeled as controlling, a wet blanket, or a nag. Rationalizations for enabling an alcoholic partner may range from telling yourself that it is the kind thing to do or that he or she really did need help to saying that you needed to protect the kids. It is embarrassing to have an alcoholic partner, it isn't a good example for the kids, it will consume your money, and you may lose friends over it.

> Stop protecting your alcoholic loved one from the harsh consequences that he or she should be facing himself or herself.

The tide of problems that you have been trying to hold back with the hard work of unhealthy enabling will only stay for a while. Eventually, you will need to admit that the alcoholism is a real problem that needs pubic attention and let the alcoholic make his or her poor decisions and, as they say, "hit rock bottom" to realize what he or she is missing. Stop protecting your alcoholic loved one from the harsh consequences that he or she should be facing himself or herself. Alcoholics need enablers to protect them from the consequences in order to remain alcoholics; if the alcoholic has to face the consequences for himself or herself in their most brutal forms, they are much more likely to quit. The alcoholic has to take responsibility for himself or herself and not blame others for hard times and severe consequences.

Story of Alcoholism in the Military Family's Home

Here is a story that is not uncommon in a military family with an alcoholic member; perhaps you have friends or family who might act similarly. Your husband comes home from a long week of work in the field doing training exercises. It's the weekend, and his friends are calling him to go drinking. You tell him that the kids miss him, that there isn't much money left in the account, and that you had hoped he would quit drinking. He tells you that he will be home tomorrow to spend time with the family and that he needs to get out and forget his problems for a while and that you worry too much. In the middle of the night while you are sleeping, you get a call from your husband at the bar; your husband's designated driver drank too much and now your husband needs a ride. You are tired yourself from caring for the kids all day, but he begs you to pick him up and reminds you that at least he isn't drunk driving. You are grateful that he didn't get in a fight like he did last week and that you didn't have to bail him out of jail like your neighbor had to do. You swear to him that this is the last time! You change clothes, drive down, and have a friend watch the house while the kids are sleeping. At home, he stumbles over the doorway and falls face first on the kitchen floor. He's got a big bump on his head now, and he's rolling over and puking on himself as he passes out. You moan as you realize that you're going to have to clean him. You pull him up the stairs, clean up his vomit, wash his clothes, drag him through the shower, change his clothes, and tuck him into bed with a soft, fluffy comforter pulled up to his chin.

He wakes up the next morning, touches the bump on his head, and turns to face you. "Thank you, honey, I couldn't live without you. You are an angel," he mutters with an obvious head-ache, but he manages a smile to show his gratitude. You touch the bump on his head lovingly and kiss his head. *How do other spouses deal with this?* you think as you walk out the door. He has told you that other service members drink way more than him. You resent him, and this isn't what you wanted in a marriage, but he's right; he couldn't live without you. On some level it feels good to be needed. He probably wouldn't have got that promotion to corporal if you hadn't pushed him to get it, and without you he might have even been kicked out of the service for all the problems he's gotten into and you bailed him out from. Even as you resent him, you may feel slightly proud of yourself for your hard work and that he at least appreciates you, which is a much better experience than when he is mad and calls names.

Now, let's look at things from the alcoholic's perspective. He has a tough week at work, and he complains regularly about it to you. You are appreciative of his hard work and everything he puts up with. He knows you don't like his drinking, and he has to put up with your nagging, but in the end, you still tuck him in at night with a fluffy comforter and pajamas he didn't even put on. His teeth are brushed and his throw up is gone. He never has to suffer any real consequences of drinking alcohol because you protected him from them as much as you could.

The relationship is codependent because he swears he can't live without you (an unhealthy emotional dependence), and you work tirelessly to please him (more unhealthy reliance on his approval). You will need to start looking for ways to boost your self-esteem by setting healthy boundaries and simply fulfilling your own responsibilities if you are ever going to get out of the cycle you are in of guilting him and feeling guilty yourself.

Tough love insists that in the story above, the wife should have let her husband stay at the bar, and if she is fearful that he will come home and berate or hurt her, she should call the police or take her family somewhere safe. The best time to avoid a code-pendent relationship is right at the beginning by making it clear that you will not bail your partner out figuratively or literally from his or her bad choices when he or she drinks alcohol or purposefully acts irresponsibly. If you are already in a relationship in which you have bailed out a family member numerous times, seek help and support. Take a stand for what will keep you and your family safe.

Let's rewrite the story above. You refuse to pick your husband up from the bar, but somehow he makes it home (e.g., called a taxi) and trips onto the kitchen floor. You come check his pulse, make sure he doesn't choke on his vomit, and check for serious injuries, then perhaps put a blanket on him. Stop there. When he wakes up in the morning, he will be in serious pain lying on the kitchen floor. The children may find him in a heap and wonder why he is there. Don't bail him out. Tell them that their father came home and that is where he collapsed. You don't need to explain anything. Let him do the explaining when he wakes up. He won't want to go drink again after a humiliating night like that.

> ## Take a stand for what will keep you and your family safe.

If he wakes up with a migraine, he may say, "I should stop drinking." You say, "That's a good idea! What can I do to help?" You don't change his clothes, clean him up, tuck him in, or do anything that will prevent him from suffering nonlethal natural consequences. If he threatens suicide, call the police. If he threatens divorce, tell him you'll help him fill out the papers. If he says he'll kill you, get the kids and get out of the house and to a domestic violence shelter.

If you are afraid to do these things, look closer at what is motivating you. Do you get angry when people *criticize* how you try to help your partner? Are you *annoyed* by your partner's selfish behavior yet blame others when he does something irresponsible? Do you feel *guilty* about covering up for your partner's behavior? Are you fearful someone's *eyes* will open up to the tough situation you're in and confront your enabling behavior? If so, perhaps you're in a CAGE codependent relationship. Perhaps you've become as dependent on him or her as he or she is on you. You've become dependent on your partner on some level; he or she has made your self-esteem or perceived self-worth dependent on whether he or she approves of how you help him or her. When your partner said he or she couldn't live without you, maybe it made you glad to have his or her approval. Maybe you feel horrible when he or she disapproves of your failure to protect him or her from consequences. The truth is that your emotions shouldn't be dependent on your partner's approval or disapproval. You need to get back to having independent emotions that are not reactive to your partner's emotions. If you are fearful to express your own emotions lest your partner get angry, that's a bad sign. Feeling safe in your relationship should be a priority for everyone. Once you have that, you can do some relationship enhancement, and your partner can start being responsible for his or her own emotions and actions rather than blaming them on you or someone else.

Let me share one more story of how I've seen this play out successfully. A woman wearing threadbare clothing and without a scrap of makeup or any other accessory for herself came into counseling and said that she was severely depressed. When asked about her life, she sounded like a responsible person. Her counselor identified something was wrong in the family, and after questioning her about it, she reluctantly answered in the affirmative. She was a stay-at-home mom who took care of the children while her husband worked long hours in the military. He made plenty of money, but he drank up their money most nights, ignored the kids or yelled at them, and complained of his wife's nagging. She said that she had no money for diapers or baby food, yet they made enough money that they didn't qualify for food stamps. The wife took her counselor's advice and went to an off-base Al-Anon meeting (a nationwide organization for family members of alcoholics) where she met some wonderful women with almost identical stories. She realized that being a military wife did not mean that she had to do whatever her husband asked of her to promote his job just because she relied on his paycheck. Six months later (a minimum time requirement from my experience), her husband had gotten help for his alcoholism and counseling for his lack of family skills. He was helping with chores around the house, going to church with his wife, performing his work functions with less complaining, and being a loving husband who stayed home with the family or took her out on dates on weekends. During those six months, her counselor coached her every step of the way. As she learned principles from the counselor and her new friends at Al-Anon, she didn't hesitate to apply them. She stopped trying to make him do or not do anything or be anything, and she didn't back down to his coercion, except when his, her, or the children's physical safety was in question. She had to go live with her mother for a short time, and at one point he went home to his own mother, who tried to enable him for a while, but eventually she, too, got tired of his problems and sent him home.

The wife learned to be independent, and she wasn't afraid of letting her husband suffer consequences, even if it meant that she suffered with him. The difference was that her suffering was not from lying to cover up for him; it came from sorrowing that he was making bad choices.

Interdependence Is the Answer

Stephen R. Covey, in his book *The 7 Habits of Highly Effective Families*, says the healthiest relationship is interdependence. It has components of dependence and independence. Imagine the two small circles again from the start of the chapter, with you and your partner as stick figures inside them; each small circle acts as a little dominion of independence. Now draw a big circle around both the smaller circles. This is what interdependence looks like.

You still act independently, but you just increased your domain, and now you share some jobs with your partner: chores, kids, sociality, bills, errands, shopping, etc. If one of you doesn't do your share, you both suffer; if you both hold up your end, you both rejoice. Folks say it isn't fair that their partners can threaten to leave them homeless, abuse them, or manipulate them because their partners bring home the money and have the most power. Yes, that behavior is abusive, but you were tricked, and your partner didn't hold up his or her end of the bargain that was dependent on both of you. Now you need to weigh your options and stop protecting your partner from what you are both about to suffer because of his or her choices. If you call the police on your partner because of abuse and he or she tries to blame you, then he or she is wrong. If your partner loses rank because you told on him or her for abusing you, remember that it was your partner's choice to abuse you in the first place.

Everyone makes their own choices, and how other people respond is their choice. You are just making a choice to protect yourself. If your partner threatens to make you pay because you told his or her command about the abuse at home, you should tell the command about that, too. There are victim advocates, case managers, and therapists all over every US base throughout the world that are just waiting to help you.

These principles apply to parents and alcoholic teenagers as well, and military parents should not cover up for their child's bad choices just because it might reflect poorly on them. Don't bail them out—chastise them at home. Kids will learn that you aren't really just concerned about your public appearance. Children should be made to suffer appropriate consequences no matter what age they may be. If it was a public choice, it should have a public consequence. Children learn to differentiate rewards and punishments just like adults and need appropriate caring and responsible role models to follow.

Summary

Alcoholism is a major issue in the military and culturally is often enabled both on-base and off-base. Every family should be concerned about what effect this will have on them. Outside professional help should be sought immediately if there appears to be significant risk for a family member, and the CAGE questions can help you determine that risk level. Acting independently and seeking help is a good start for building emotional independence in your relationship, an essential ingredient to a healthy interdependent relationship. Codependence is a poor way of trying to save yourself and your partner from consequences or suffering by trying to cover up your partner's mistakes. Most military commands are going to be understanding of service members who take preventative steps to avoid alcohol-related incidents because such incidents reflect poorly on them, too. Every base has alcohol-specific treatment clinics and counselors.

Interdependence is a healthy way of acknowledging and allowing the suffering and recognizing suffering as a normal consequence of poor decisions. Interdependence is maintaining your independence to make healthy choices regardless of what your partner chooses or how much he or she might reject your choice. Interdependence is respecting one another's independence. It is living your life as strongly as you did when you were single, but now you've got a second job—taking care of your family.

Stuck in the Sand: Isolation and Suicide

Down here in Twentynine Palms, California, it is not unusual to see cars up to their axles in sand. It's pretty funny when you're driving by, but it's not so funny when it's your car several miles off the main road. Fortunately, I had cell phone reception and a friend with a big truck when I got stuck. Our family had decided to drive off into the desert down a twisting sand road, but when I went off the main road to turn around, our all-wheel-drive van sank deeper and deeper into the earth with each of our attempts to free ourselves. We told the kids it was an adventure and that scraping around the wheels with our bare hands was like digging at the beach! An attempt to lay rocks behind the wheel after digging around the tires proved fruitless. When our friend's giant white Chevy truck came down the desert road, our friend looked like an angel in a four by four. One torn strap later, we successfully pulled out, leaving a huge, gaping hole where the front right tire had been spinning.

Suicide is on the rise in the military, and families are left without a husband or wife, father or mother. Perhaps these souls could have been helped, or perhaps not, but I can't help but wonder if they felt as helpless as I did when I tried to get my van out of the sand. No matter how hard they hit the gas, they just dug deeper. The coping skills they had used all their lives weren't working. They tried going forward and in reverse, but they felt like they were alone in the desert. Feeling isolated or actually being isolated is a profile for suicide risk; if individuals don't feel like they have someone to talk to, or they aren't willing to talk, their risk increases. A service member described to me that it felt like his entire life was falling apart around him. He had lost a significant person in his life, and now he doubted all the religious beliefs he had learned as a child. Several medical problems from his years of service kept him in chronic pain and prevented him from exercising sufficiently to keep his weight within the required limits. Serious financial issues on top of awkward social skills and family problems at home made him a high risk for suicide from a counselor's point of view. He had no close friends on base and no family in the state, leaving him feeling isolated and stranded in a culture that he felt like had rejected him because of his mental and physical limitations. Serious traumatic memories from his past had brought him into counseling, and his anger issues were so severe that he would regularly rage in the counseling room and slam doors or make verbal threats against anyone who verbally questioned him. Surprisingly, he adamantly denied ever having any suicidal thoughts. Positive resolutions did gradually come to this marine's life, but it was slow going. Being alone can make a person feel desperate and could explain why both single and divorced soldiers were found to have twice the rate of suicide following a deployment to Afghanistan or Iraq

Don't hesitate to intervene in someone's life in a positive and inspirational way.

compared to those who are married. This service member, like others, rarely had profound experiences in my office, but he did return each time saying that just being listened to and cared about made him feel safe enough to keep trying and not do anything he would seriously regret.

I don't think many suicides occur in the early morning hours, because things always look better then. Life is more tolerable when you see a new sun rising. Most suicides occur at night, when you're tired and worn and you should be sleeping but you can't figure out how to get through the pain. If you think you should intervene in someone's life in a positive and inspirational way, don't hesitate. Now, if your attempt to be positive and inspirational is really inspired by selfish hopes of getting your friend or family member to stop moaning and groaning and it actually makes them feel worse, take a step back and learn how to care. Shaming another person into action may make the tires spin faster, but it doesn't dig them out. My friend with the truck, who pulled me out, arrived quickly when I called for help. He reassured me that I wasn't a complete idiot when he said, "If you're in the desert, you're gonna get stuck eventually." He normalized the problem and taught me that my getting stuck wasn't because I was just ignorant or stupid. We live in a desert, and the sand can look deceivingly sturdy when it's not. All of us occasionally make bad turns, pull off to rest, or have lapses in good judgment. My friend knew I didn't need chastening; he knew that getting stuck in sand was always a possibility and a danger. Most people who make bad decisions already know they are bad decisions, but at that moment people make them they seem like the right decisions. Service members may know that drugs and alcohol have destroyed other people's lives and that their teachers, mentors, and command representatives have warned them against these addictive substances, but at the time it seems like the best way to pull out of the sand. If I was fearful my friend would just come and berate me or make my tires keep spinning, I wouldn't have called him. Perhaps this fear of being ridiculed prevents some service members from seriously seeking help when they are feeling suicidal and stuck.

The service member I described above actually had several acquaintances in the military commit suicide, and each time it happened, he would go into a deep sadness. He described with anger how some of the senior command indirectly referred to the service member or anyone that committed suicide as weak and unworthy of further discussion. This mind-set, of course, is not in harmony with the true ideals of the military when compared to mottos like "Never Leave a Marine Behind," which is the course name for the suicide-prevention training among marines. Finding the balance between pushing someone to the limits and showing them mercy is a difficult leadership skill and requires that a person be sensitive to where the limit lies with each individual.

> Find the balance between pushing someone to the limits and mercy— be sensitive to where the limit lies with each individual.

Spinning your wheels in the sand is probably a result of several things happening in your life. I think of people as having many dimensions and arenas in their life: work, school, family, friends, social life, finances, past problems, punishments, legal issues, and religious or spiritual problems can all add up. If just one or two of these arenas take on some substantial stressors, we can usually take care of them; if all of them are moderately high, we can usually lower them and see a way out. But when all are moderate to high, and even one or two spike higher than ever, we may feel like we are up to our necks in suffocating sand. A citation for driving while intoxicated could make people feel suicidal and want to give up, or it could act as an impetus that awakens them to their awful situations and inspires them to change their lives for the better. The difference could be as simple as someone being there to offer a hand and show them a more excellent way than taking their own lives.

Summary

Prior to 2001, the active-duty suicide rate was lower than the civilian rate, but then it doubled in the middle of the war and has continued to rise with a record high in 2012. If you even think that a family member may be at risk for suicide, ask him or her directly if he or she is thinking about it, assess for plans, and find out if he or she has a means to commit suicide. If his or her report sounds at all disturbing to you, go to the emergency room or a counselor for crisis counseling. Some people fear that asking questions about suicide will cause the person questioned to start thinking about committing suicide, but it actually shows care and concern and can act as a preventative and help the person know that you are paying attention.

14

Anger, Abuse, and Killing

In the military, anger is a common emotion. Whether it's screaming and swearing and kicking trashcans across the office or icy
cold anger, each terrifies subordinates. Killing and destroying
(often associated with anger) is what service members are trained
to do. This is exemplified by one bumper sticker I saw when I was
on a marine base which read, "If it absolutely positively has to
be destroyed today: US Marines." From the day that recruits are
brought to boot camp or basic training, there is in-your-face yelling
and instant anger whenever mistakes are made. Drill instructors
and drill sergeants work hard to be as intimidating as possible.
A friend of mine who had served in the military for several years
before getting married told me that he was so accustomed to
yelling whenever he got slightly upset that he had a hard time
adjusting when he got home with his wife. Another friend pointed
out that when he yelled at home, it terrified his wife, but he didn't

think he was even yelling compared to what he experienced while serving in the US Marines.

Anger as a Mood-Altering Activity

We all know about how alcohol alters one's mood or how drugs in general, including prescription drugs, can change one's entire mood, outlook, perspective, and general well-being with just a few specks of dust in a pill. They can make an uptight person lose his or her inhibition, fine motor functioning, and ability to distinguish fantasy from reality. Anger has the same capacity to alter one's state of being. Some people don't even think of anger as a pure emotion in itself because it seems to always follow other more pure emotions like sadness and fear. As a secondary emotion, anger may be more of a defense mechanism (and it's hard to be defensive without being offensive). The anger serves as a tool for at least one of two purposes:

1. to alter our mood when we experience an unwanted emotion like sadness, fear, embarrassment, humiliation, confusion, or grief
2. to fulfill one's feelings of entitlement

I've seen people use anger as a mood-altering tool; one person should have been crying about his or her mother dying but instead became furious and angry. Anger is more readily accepted in hypermasculine environments like the military, while sadness is often labeled a sign of weakness. Sadness often follows feelings of loss and includes the physical sensation of emptiness and darkness inside, which for many people is uncomfortable and undesired. Anger can be chosen as an emotion to replace an undesired emotion—but it comes at a cost.

The choice to be angry alters our mood physiologically because millions of nerve endings in the body send out adrenaline, noradrenaline, and other heart-pumping, muscle-clenching chemicals all over the body. For most people, their heart rate doubles when they are angry, and their blood pressure almost doubles.

Consequences of anger may also include lasting bodily effects like headaches, muscles spasms, chest pains, stomach problems, proneness to ulcers, greater likelihood of getting sick, hormonal imbalances, and sugar deficiencies. Eknath Easwaran paraphrases Buddha and says that "we are not punished for our anger; we are punished by our anger."

Individuals on the receiving end of hostility and anger have temporary anxiety, but anger and hostility in its express-er can cause more permanent effects, like heart attacks, strokes, and overall declining health (a review of some of these articles and my research can be found in my dissertation, "Hostility in Marital Interaction, Depressive Symptoms, and Physical Health of Husbands and Wives"). Talking to retired service members and observing their active-duty counterparts, I have come to believe that getting angry regularly will take a toll on one's life physically, emotionally, and mentally.

Anger as a Barrier to Communication

When you are experiencing an emotion, you are experiencing your body trying to tell you something. Listening to active-duty service members converse with one another and talking to them in private, I found that the most frequently communicated emotion was anger. People are always influencing one another with their emotions. Think of the last time you walked into a room with a bunch of nervous and angry people; it was probably hard to main-tain any other emotion in yourself but anger and nervousness. What about when you walked into a room full of people giving a surprise birthday party? It's hard to not be happy with them. Our energy states or emotional settings are contagious. I believe that service members who are able to purposefully and con-sciously choose emotions and mindsets other than anger will be able to communicate a lot better with their family members and feel more fulfilled and satisfied with their overall work, life, and relationships.

In order for military family members to communicate better with one another, they will have to first learn to understand and accept their own emotional communications. The next time you get angry at someone, try to consciously consider whether or not there are underlying emotions contributing to the anger. Try using HeartMath to dissipate the anger and then, with your clear mindset, consider if there are other underlying factors contributing to your anger. Maybe you made a choice years ago to get angry if someone disrespected you a certain way. Friends, family, and society may have taught you what constituted disrespect or a violation of your entitlements and how to retaliate with anger. In the military, there may be unspoken traditions of when it is OK to get angry and when it is unacceptable.

One service member who got in trouble for retaliating at his wife's anger told me, "My lieutenant says that I need to keep my wife on a shorter leash. He says that my wife gets away with too much." Numerous other service members expressed rage when another service member dressed in any way that was out of alignment with dress requirements, like missing a belt loop or failing to cut a thread off the uniform. Getting angry about these seemingly small problems was strange to me and other civilians, but not to the service members who believed it was a sign of sloppiness

> Learn to understand and accept your own emotional communications.

and reflected poorly on every other marine or sailor. Fortunately, each person understood this underlying assumption, and they were usually able to not take it personally. I asked men in my domestic violence prevention class how they let their wives know they were angry. They usually said that at first they would sulk, huff, and *act* angry by moving abruptly or not making eye contact and breathing heavily. My next question was, "What can your wife do to make you not angry at that point?" The answers varied, but ultimately it came down to the wife having to satisfy his demands or appease him in some manner. The man's anger usually blinded the man to how his wife might perceive him, what her needs might be, and how his anger could be damaging the relationship.

If their wives did not appease them, most men acknowledged that they would then step it up. Sometimes they would explode in anger, and other times they would hold it in for weeks before an explosion or some other form of retaliatory anger. If the man does explode in anger, can he really blame his wife for his explosion? The common myth is that we just explode because there are too many problems in our lives to cope with and the steam boils over, or the water flows over the brim of the cup. If that were true, then we would always be able to predict when people were about to spill over, but we can't. What I think is really happening is that the person who is angry is actually turning up the heat until the matter is resolved how he or she wants it to be. No matter what the person he or she is angry with says, the angry person can twist it around to become increasingly angry. The anger will keep increasing, perhaps for years, until he or she explodes.

What really needs to happen in a situation like this is that the angry person should learn to regulate his or her own emotions. It is one person's job to regulate your emotions—your own. Otherwise, you will find yourself always waiting for others to regulate your emotions for you by changing what they think, say, and do to appease you. That would be a powerless feeling in which you don't have control of your own emotions. You may even start to feel more disrespected because the other person isn't paying enough attention to your emotions.

A healthier relationship will include both partners actively taking responsibility of their own emotions but paying enough attention to the partner's emotions so neither partner's emotions are prioritized over the other's. For example, one partner should not get angry at another partner for getting angry, and neither partner should use his or her anger to intimidate the other partner into submission.

Being angry is kind of like being hypnotized; you may be used to instantly getting angry over a small thing. Deprogramming yourself from the anger and reprogramming yourself with more positive and accepting emotions will take practice and careful analysis and lots of patience with yourself. Your family members will greatly appreciate every effort you make to minimize your anger and increase your understanding.

Love and Anger

When asked, a service member would usually say that he or she wants his or her wife or husband and children to be motivated by love in his or her words and actions toward them. Of course, when the question is turned, few people can genuinely say they usually have these same emotions occurring in their daily interactions with family members. Too often we are caught up in getting our own needs met without considering how we are impacting others. When you are faced with a difficult family situation, repeat to yourself the mantra "Love is always the answer." If family members can feel your love, even in a stern rebuke or in a hug afterwards, they will be more likely to follow through on your requests, and your relationship will improve.

The second mantra you may want to remind yourself of in family relationships is "If I'm angry, I'm wrong." Choosing to be angry in your family interactions is like choosing junk food rather than healthy fruits and vegetables. Anger is a poor substitute for patience and caring and may only provide temporary satiation and unwanted side effects. If you are in a committed relationship, temporary fixes are not good enough. Demanding instant compliance through anger may be a symptom of your own selfishness. You may rationalize your impatience, saying that you are really working for the greater good when you rush a family member, but unless you are escaping a fire, you are probably lacking the even bigger picture—that kids don't respond well to impatience.

Think of the last time you tried to rush your kids to get ready. The result was probably crying children, forgotten items, and mismatched clothes. Investing more energy into your children requires patience, time, and energy. Sacrifices on your part may include getting up a little earlier (or staying up later), not taking as long of a shower, teaching your kids how to get themselves ready the day before, and carefully evaluating problems before deciding to get upset and rush. To sum it up, anger

> When you are faced with a difficult family situation, repeat to yourself the mantra "Love is always the answer."

and impatience are closely tied together, and both lead to greater overall anxiety. Developing a more loving approach includes losing the anger toward the people you love. If you want, save that anger for an attacking bear or someone who is really physically threatening you.

Abuse in Military Families

Working in the Family Advocacy Program, I saw a lot of couples and families come into counseling because of allegations of abuse. The abuse rarely included serious physical injury, but the psychological injuries were often deep and severe. The victims often broke down crying while telling their stories of humiliation and abuse. Offenders rarely had insight into why they acted as they did or what impact they had on their partners or why it was even a problem. Sometimes they even saw themselves as more like victims. Unfortunately, multiple deployments may actually be increasing the chance of child abuse and neglect in families. Abuse in relationships is a terrible thing and is, in my opinion, the result of not being sensitive enough to other people's feelings. Respect is absolutely demanded of subordinates in the military, but in my opinion, it is not always reciprocated by superiors when they yell obscenities at subordinates for their mistakes. I am not criticizing their methods, which may be necessary, but this approach definitely won't work in a family.

Respect between family members is an essential ingredient to happy relationships. Inflated perceptions of how much respect we feel we deserve compared to the respect we show others could be a contributing factor to unhappy families and abuse (See Lundy Bancroft's book *Why Does He Do That? Inside the Minds of Angry and Controlling Men*). If one partner believes he or she is above criticism but criticizes others, he or she has set double standards that he or she may even refuse to acknowledge. Children may not have the same level of entitlement as adults, and they may not be able to articulate their needs clearly, but their needs should never be neglected because of adult wants. Small children are terrified by loud noises, and angry yelling is no exception.

Killing

Murder is a terrible thing, but killing in the military is not the same as murder. Many people pressed into service in Germany during World War II were forced to fight for Hitler, despite hating him. These people either killed or were killed, despite possibly even wanting the opposition to win. The depth of an act is often only known to those who have committed it. Haunting feelings may follow those who have had to kill in combat. Even as a therapist, I did not ask service members if they "ever killed someone." This is a common (but insensitive) question that service members are generally uncomfortable answering for many reasons.

I have seen individuals who wanted to kill and came back sickened by the act. While working in the Deployment Health Clinical Center, therapists regularly recommended that those who actually enjoyed the act of killing be separated from the military. The five-star book *On Killing: The Psychological Cost of Learning to Kill in War and Society* details the psychological affects that killing has on people: feelings of worthlessness are not uncommon, accompanied by depression and extreme regret. The most devastated service members were those who had to kill a child suicide bomber. When these acts are properly framed in the context of one's duty in war, these individuals can return to a more normal life, but it should not be assumed that it will be the same life they left. Many say that they will never look at another human being in quite the same way. A healthy change will include treasuring human life more than ever after seeing it disappear so quickly. Guilty feelings should be differentiated from destructive self-blaming and shaming feelings. Service members can grow as a result of their experiences and become wise beyond their years and more merciful than ever in the right context.

> Be patient with yourself and find others that have been through what you've been through; talk to them and find out what has worked for them.

Be patient with yourself and find others that have been through what you've been through; talk to them and find out what has worked for them. Whatever you do, don't write yourself off or allow yourself to sink into shame any longer. Remind yourself that it was your duty, or at least what you believed was your duty at the time. If bad choices were made, recognize them as only bad choices and not as the result of you being a bad person. Process the memories in a healthy way with someone you trust. Talk, write, and meditate deeply about the memories from your deployment. Again, sadness is a common and good emotion. If you can find a safe place to express sadness, you should let it be expressed freely through tears. These acts allow you to become more conscious and aware of what actually took place. A greater awareness leads to greater insight and acceptance. Ultimately, you must accept yourself as a valid human being who deserves to live and find joy, whether or not you agree with what you actually did or did not do. The emotions associated with the memories may be overpowering, but the emotions are temporal and changing. Appropriate processing of the emotions will change them into positive emotions that motivate you to perhaps sacrifice more and live with greater mercy and love. Hiding the memories from yourself is a game that doesn't last and is foolish; it would be like trying to push a cork down in water that only comes up more forcefully with each shove.

Summary

While anger is a common emotion in our society, and especially in military settings, it is generally overused and usually detrimental when used in families. Anger is often a block to communication between family members and prevents people from being able to process what others are saying and what emotions they are actually experiencing. Service members may be in the habit of becoming angry and yelling in their work setting and have difficulty transitioning to more loving emotions at home. Anger is a frequent co-occurring emotion with violence and abuse, but is never an excuse for such behavior and is generally counterproductive in creating healthy family relationships. Killing is a necessity in many service members' deployments and can require serious reflection and processing afterwards. Family members should make every attempt to be sensitive to one another's emotions and avoid double standards of allowing themselves to get angry while forbidding others to get angry. Children should be nurtured and loved with patience and not yelled at in anger. Anger is generally the result of years of habituation and may require intensive study and processing in a professional setting before individuals can transform its use into more positive experiences.

Death and Spiritual Coping

Almost everyone in the military will be affected by death at some point. Military family members may witness death, consider death themselves, cause death, or lose friends and family to death. Whether you are religious and attend church or not is irrelevant in processing death through a spiritual lens. Spirituality is like any other dimension of a person's life: if it is ignored long enough, it will only exacerbate your life overall. It is like trying to ignore the tires on a car but fixing every other part of the vehicle. Spirituality is what grounds you; it is where the rubber hits the road. This may sound contrary to what you imagine in terms of spirituality being an uplifting presence. Think of it as the string on a kite that keeps it up by giving it roots to the ground or as the unseen air in expanded tires.

I attended a funeral service for one of my clients while on base, and I was amazed at the spirit I felt. I sat in the back to avoid being conspicuous and to observe. When they played taps and then did roll call, many people in the congregation began crying. The roll call included people answering until they got to the deceased member's name; they called it out several times with no answer. It was haunting how silent the room was, and as I recall it now, it still brings tears to my eyes. I recalled how, in our last session together, the service member had found himself caught up in the culture of death; he had done some things he was not proud of while deployed. His peers and command all loved and respected him, but he was struggling with which way to turn as he had reached a crossroad. I held up for him a crayon picture that my four-year-old daughter had drawn the week before. It included a rainbow and our family smiling as different colored stick figures. I knew that he as an artist would appreciate its beautiful simplicity and emotion. I knew that he as a parent would feel a hiccup in his heart as he thought of how his own daughter saw the world compared to how he saw it.

Is it possible that as we grow older we deny the spirituality present in a rainbow and the closeness of family? We get caught up instead in the media-driven success market of how well we perform in work, sports, school, hobbies, or earning potential. I have the rainbow picture on my wall to remind me of this spiritual experience. Many of the principles explained in this book and used by therapists have their origins in earlier spiritual pioneers' teachings. These principles help people find enlightenment and joy in their lives.

Reminders of Loved Ones

Whether you believe in an afterlife or not, perhaps you at least believe that deceased comrades will live on in your and other's memories. In Twentynine Palms, the marines often wear metal wristbands that have the names of their fallen comrades etched in them. At first, these bands were questioned as unsuitable to wear with the uniform, but eventually it was allowed. I think it was recognized as a means of healing and accepting loss. These marines were not avoiding the loss in their life; they were reminding themselves of it whenever they glanced at or moved their hands. They had faith that they could heal from the emotional pain of losing someone and the sadness and hurt, even if they never forgot it. If you've ever seen the Vietnam War Memorial, then you know how spiritually poignant and sacred a name can be when etched into stone. Many battalions have similar shrines in their hallways with images of fallen soldiers and marines and their names displayed on walls to remind one another of things that can't be articulated any other way. Often found near these memorials are battle crosses that include boots, a rifle and bayonet, dog tags, and a helmet.

Whether in the field or in a church on base, service members are welcome to have an opening prayer or invocation when conducting memorial ceremonies. Churches, religion, spirituality, and chaplains of every faith have always been associated with soldiers and armies since the start of civilization and are often stabilizing forces for service men and women.

I had the opportunity to speak with the wife of the deceased marine I mentioned earlier. She explained how her whole perception of life changed at his death. Before, she had believed that there was no spirit in a person and that once someone died, that was the end of them. However, when she looked on her husband's deceased corpse, she realized that it was as if he had left and all that remained was a shell of the man she knew. She described what a spiritual experience it was to spread her husband's ashes over a body of water and know that her husband's wishes had been granted. Keeping the memories and spirits of loved ones in our minds and hearts by some means or another is, for many, a spiritual connection that motivates us to go on and pursue good goals in memory of our loved ones.

Spirituality as a Dimension of Self

Don't categorize yourself as spiritual or nonspiritual. Take the time to just exist. Victor Frankl, a concentration camp survivor, would suggest that you search for meaning in your life. Searching for the meaning in your life is actually meaningful in itself. I don't know for sure how spirituality is different from emotionality and mentality; they seem to be closely tied and overlap with one another like every other part of our persona. No two people will agree on everything discussed that is spiritual because everyone's experiences are unique to them and their culture. A self-described Wiccan, who was also a marine, told me that he read from the Devil's Bible. This was a little jolting

> Fulfill your spiritual needs by seeking out spiritual texts, talking to people that you are spiritually attracted to, finding a group that encourages discussion of people's spiritual sides, and finding time to reflect alone in silence.

to my Christian upbringing, but we were able to find common ground because he believed that people should treat one another kindly and seek to find beautiful things around them. Spirituality is full of paradoxes, and most religious doctrines preach principles to guide people in their lives.

Spirituality for Adjusting Service Members

An insightful marine who felt powerless in his new work identified for me one of these spiritual paradoxes. He had grown up in a home full of abuse, fear, and intimidation. Now he wanted to be powerful, but he felt powerless to get along with other marines. We talked for hours, and he concluded weeks later that humility was the way to power. He explained, "There are differences between those with real power and those with fake power. Only the meek have power. You can tell when people are just in it for themselves. No one wants to follow them. Their leadership and authority is only by name, whereas the leader who cares about his or her unit is willing to take correction and be teachable—the essence of humility."

Homesick

Living in a place far from home, especially in a desert, can be a scary experience. If you didn't grow up in a desert, it is probably vastly different from wherever you are from. Twentynine Palm's Mojave Desert is nigh unto identical to the Afghanistan desert, full of scraggly bushes, sand, and bare brown mountains. The emptiness can be haunting, but it can also be a place to search one's soul. Many of the most spiritual people in history have spent some portion of their lives in the desert wilderness, wandering around until they found their way. Enlisted service members that live in barracks or dorms often do not have cars to get off base and have few if any friends off base. They rarely have any good reasons to leave the base and often come into counseling because they are homesick and tired of the total military immersion. I would encourage them to walk into the hills and put some distance between themselves and the base and then sit and wait and meditate and/or pray. Sometimes these service members would return with stories about how they felt lighter and had clarity of mind.

Coping with Past Deaths

A service member who had lost a close family member in a tragic and violent incident came in to see me and said that he was numb. He reported that life was too hard for him, and no matter what he did, bad things kept happening. He was depressed and not sleeping well. Together we identified what he was thankful for, what good things had already happened to him, and what good things he wanted to see happen in the future.

"What do you want out of counseling?" I asked him.

"I want to have emotions again," he answered.

When people speak of spiritual experiences, they usually say that they *felt* something spiritual. In this man's case, he and his family member had previously been very active in a church and shared many spiritual experiences together when singing hymns and playing music together. The years of hardship he had seen in the service and his feelings of loss had caused him to cut himself off from his past, his emotions, and his spiritual connections to life and people around him. To him, talking to others and having friends was a spiritual experience and helped bind his pain. Using some HeartMath techniques, he was able to connect in his heart with the deceased family member. He sat and cried through the intense sadness of losing her, even after years of other times crying, but this time he had welcomed the spiritual connection that accompanied the experience.

In my second session with a marine who was struggling with increased irritability with his newlywed, he began crying within five minutes of practicing just paying attention to his heart. For the rest of the session, this marine cried quietly with his eyes closed as he listened to what his heart had to tell him. "I haven't paid attention to my heart in a long time," he said. "I've just been stuck in my brain and sad since my father's death." The service member described how he went from sadness to happiness and then back again; with each new emotional cycle, he would return to the image of his beautiful bride the first time he saw her walk down the aisle of their wedding. This marine's spiritual recollections of committing his life to another person helped him process his father's death from years before.

Memories really can be haunting, but perhaps they are ghosts that have a story and a message they are trying to tell or teach. Listen to your body and pay attention to what you feel. Don't water down the feelings with mood-altering substances. Get a relationship with yourself. If relationships are spiritual connections between two people, perhaps you need to create a better relationship with your *own* soul first and not be afraid of what it is has to tell you.

Be-Do-Have Creation Cycle

In the armed forces, individuals sign up knowing that it is possible that duty will call them to sacrifice their lives. Many are prepared for this, but few are prepared to sacrifice and lose those they labor beside. A man, whom we'll call Herman, came in for counseling because he couldn't seem to pull himself back together, and he wondered if I could help him. His close biological brother had been killed earlier, he had some symptoms of PTSD himself, he was divorced with custody problems, he had lost rank because of the dishonesty of another, and he was struggling with regaining his prior status in the service. Herman explained that he used to *have* it all, but now he had lost everything. My assessment was that he was in a deep spiritual crisis. He was so focused on how he wanted to *have* these things back that he couldn't focus on anything else.

"You're stuck in the *do* phase," I told him.

"What do you mean?" he said, looking at me as if I were crazy.

"You keep trying to *do* things to make your life better. You used to *have* a lot of stuff because you would *do* a lot of things, so you're trying to *do* it all over again thinking you'll get the same results, and you're surprised that you aren't."

"So what do I *do*?" he asked, more interested.

"You have to just *be*. Don't *do* anything. Just *be*."

The marine was having a hard time wrapping his mind around this, but that was the beginning of *being*. I instructed him to stop trying to get results, to stop trying to *have* more, and to just go sit and reflect and ponder on his life. In our anxiety-provoking, results-demanding society, this thought had never crossed his mind. He assumed that with more work he would get more stuff. The problem was that he was getting diminishing results. He had used up his resources. He was drained—"a shell of a man," in his own words. Herman was still motivated, but he was going in circles.

If you are familiar with the story of Steve Jobs, you know that he created the highly successful Apple company. When he retired, after earning billions of dollars, the company went into severe decline. Steve, who had been *being* for years in retirement at that point, had tuned into some new inspiration, and he had a plan. He returned to the company and created the iPod, iPhone, and iPad, essentially revolutionizing the world with his ingenious ideas. We could reason that if he had stayed in his company and never retired, he may never have been able to rejuvenate sufficiently to see a whole new plane of creative possibilities. He may have continued to just try and do the same old thing, getting diminishing results and wondering why the world had changed without him. Instead, he recreated himself. The cycle of *Be-Do-Have,* as described by Penney Peirce in her book *The Intuitive Way,* describes a process that few of us consciously implement. Herman, in this case, was able to make it a conscious decision, and he came back for a few more weeks with new insights each time of how he had been able to step back from his situation and see it with new perspective. He was able to see new possibilities as he practiced just existing and *being.* Eventually, when he had sufficient inspiration, he moved back into *doing,* and last I heard, he is *having* a lot of the results he originally envisioned. Hopefully, next time he loses what he did *have* again, he will be less reluctant to move back into the more spiritual state of *being.*

Sacred Texts

A military proverb of uncertain origin says, "There are no atheists in foxholes" because of the fear that grips soldiers whose death seems imminent. However, some marines I spoke to actually had opposite experiences and determined that there must be no God because of the horrible things they saw. In combat, you don't really have time to mourn and sort through horrors. Combat is usually brief—a few seconds, minutes, or hours, and at most a few days or weeks—followed by long, boring stints of waiting. Some service members describe the waiting on deployments as being in a prison and waiting to get out. The waiting period is a good time to tap into your spiritual side through prayer, meditation, and scripture study. You may be familiar with spiritual/ inspirational leaders who were imprisoned, like Nelson Mandela, Anwar Sadat, Sri Krishna, Mahatma Gandhi, Jesus Christ, and Joseph Smith Jr., who devoted their lives to studying sacred texts and prayer and came out of incarceration with new insights that changed the world.

Family

If you are reading this book, then I assume that you care about your family, since that is the orientation of this book. Many a good man and woman in combat zones made it through tough times by recalling sacred moments with their families or seeing images in their mind's eye of their families praying for them. Sometimes the memories that saved them were of looking into a partner's eyes and seeing eternity or seeing their children's faces. Maybe you have knelt in prayer with your family and felt a spiritual presence or connection with those you love.

Family is a sacred unit of society that has spiritual roots and spiritual purposes that most of us only occasionally take time to reflect on. Our fondest hope when we meet someone we love is to be with him or her forever, a term and a dream that would require a spiritual extension of this life. An e-mail I received at work read, "The holidays are an important time to enjoy the company of our loved ones, family, and friends and reflect on the year's successes. No marine should have to shoulder a burden alone. No marine should be left behind. Take care of each other, enjoy the well-deserved holidays, and Semper Fidelis." The brotherhood and sisterhood of the US Marines is a legacy that extends beyond the life of any single marine, and no worthy marine would take all the glory or wish for anything above his or her brothers and sisters. The same should be true in our families. We live to take care of one another. We live to give—to give to one another all we are. These are not just maxims designed to motivate; they are the emotional and spiritual roots of our human existence and are what allow us to rise above selfish actions that would only drag ourselves and the ones we care about most down. Sacrifice is the cost of cohesion between humans. Spiritual and religious doctrines rightfully identify sacrifice as an expense that makes life worthwhile.

Summary

Spirituality is a dimension of human life that is often either taken for granted, overlooked, or purposefully ignored. Service members and their families generally encounter death more often than civilians and should find healthy ways to remember loved ones and cope with serious losses. The death of a loved one is an event that causes most people to reflect seriously on spiritual and eternal matters. The best spiritual feelings often occur in our hearts, as do some of the most painful losses in our lives. Taking time to reflect on these matters can be done anywhere, including in your own home, a church, or the desert. No matter how long ago a death occurred, it can continue to haunt a person unless he or she finds ways to make peace within himself or herself through careful meditation, reading sacred texts, and seeking ways to make the world a better place in memory of loved ones.

Afterword and Acknowledgments

Being a family in the military is an exciting life experience. Whether you stay in for one enlistment or a full retirement, such a life can be enriching and supportive. Finding good friends in the military or in the community is a critical step to feeling stable and secure. I have tried to be a friend in writing this book and sharing with you some of my best advice. As a marriage and family therapist, the topics in this book address the most prevalent problems I assisted military families in overcoming.

The lives of deployed service members and their families are unlike anything else experienced in the civilian world. Families who apply the principles and advice shared in this book will have an advantage over every other family in the military. Even if your family has every problem in this book, you will find that applying the principles will help you potentially become stronger than families who have been in the military for years longer. I would love to hear from my readers and know what was helpful in this text and what you would like to see more of in future texts and editions. My thoughts are always with the families in the military who taught me and allowed me to influence their lives. I would like to acknowledge their positive service to this country and to a better world community. There are so many things that work in the military and that can be capitalized on to build successful families. I hope you will take advantage of all these structures and supports and create the family you envision through sharing, loving, and caring.

I would also like to thank my colleagues who continue to serve military families and who helped me learn the principles of military family success. The Familius family was inspiring in their mission to build happy families and make this book a reality.

References

Amato, Paul R., Alan Booth, David R. Johnson, and Stacy J. Rogers. Alone Together: How Marriage in America Is Changing. Cambridge, MA: Harvard University Press, 2007.

Anderson, Craig A., Nicholas L. Carnegey, Mindy Flanagan, Arlin J. Benjamin Jr., Janie Eubanks, and Jeffrey C. Valentine. "Violent Video Games: Specific Effects of Violent Content on Aggressive Thoughts and Behavior." Advances in Experimental Social Psychology 36, no. 1 (2004):199–249.

Bancroft, Lundy. Why Does He Do That? Inside the Minds of Angry and Controlling Men. New York: Penguin, 2002.

Brown, Genevieve Shaw. "How Much Summer Vacation $1,180 (the US Average) Can Buy." ABC News. June 7, 2012. http://abcnews.go.com/Travel/vacation-1180-buy-bargain-vacations-american-average-cost/story?id=16509865.

Buhner, Stephen Harrod. (2004). The Secret Teachings of Plants: The Intelligence of the Heart in the Direct Perception of Nature. Rochester, VT: Bear & Company, 2004.

Chapman, Gary. The Five Love Languages: The Secret to Love that Lasts. Chicago, IL: Northfield Publishing, 2009.

Childre, Doc, and Deborah Rozman. Transforming Anxiety: The Heartmath Solution for Overcoming Fear and Worry and Creating Serenity. Oakland, CA: Transforming Anxiety, 2006.

Covey, Stephen. The 7 Habits of Highly Effective Families. New York: Golden Books, 1997.

Coyne, Sarah M., Laura M. Padilla-Walker, Laura Stockdale, and Randal D. Day. "Game on Girls: Associations between Co-playing Video Games and Adolescent Behavioral and Family Outcomes." Journal of Adolescent Health 49, no. 2 (2011): 160–165.

Daily Mail Reporter. "Surfing the Internet for Long Periods of Time Can Cause Withdrawl Symptoms 'Similar to People on a Comedown from Ecstasy.'" MailOnline.com. February 17, 2013. http://www.dailymail.co.uk/news/article-2280074/

Surfing-internet-long-periods-time-cause-withdrawal-symp-
toms-similar-people-comedown-ecstasy.html.

Department of the Army. "The Soldiers Guide." Headquarters
Department of the Army. February 2004. FM 7-21.13. http://
armypubs.army.mil/doctrine/DR_pubs/dr_a/pdf/fm7_21x13.
pdf.

Divorce Statistics. "How Much Does Divorce Cost in the USA."
Divorce Statistics. http://www.divorcestatistics.info/how-
much-does-divorce-cost-in-the-usa.html.

Doherty, William. "Infidelity: After an Affair." Lakefront Well-
ness Center. 2006. http://www.lakefrontwellness.com/
wellness-topics/wt-infidelityafter.htm.

Dotinga, Randy. "Combat Vets Most Prone to Domestic Abuse:
Yale Study Looks at Homefront Effects of War on Men,
Society." National Council on Child Abuse and Family Violence. Last modified August 1, 2013. http://www.nccafv.org/
combat_vets.htm.

Easwaran, Eknath. To Love Is to Know Me: The Bhagavad Gita for
Daily Living. Berkley, CA: Blue Mountain Center of Meditation, 1984.

Eckhart, Jacey. "Young Military Marriage—Right Choice?" Mil-
itary.com. http://www.military.com/spouse/relationships/
military-marriage/young-military-marriage-right-choice.
html.

Evans, Patricia. Controlling People: How to Recognize, Understand, and Deal with People Who Try to Control You. Avon,
MA: Adams Media, 2002.

Farragut, Loyall. The Life of David Glasgow Farragut, First
Admiral of the United States Navy. New York: D. Appleton
and Company, 1879.

Foa, Edna B., Elizabeth A. Hembree, and Barbara Olasov Roth-
baum. Prolonged Exposure Therapy for PTSD: Emotional
Processing of Traumatic Experiences. New York: Oxford,
2007.

Frankl, Viktor Emil. Man's Search for Meaning. Boston, MA:
Beacon Press, 1984.

Gray, John. Men Are from Mars, Women Are from Venus. New
York: Harper Collins, 1992.

Hall, Stanley D. "Hostility in Marital Interaction, Depressive Symptoms and Physical Health of Husbands and Wives." PhD diss., Brigham Young University. June 10, 2010.

Hicks, Lundquist Jennifer. "A Comparison of Civilian and Enlisted Divorce Rates during the Early All Volunteer Force Era." Journal of Political and Military Sociology 35, no. 2 (2007):199–217.

Jacobson, Isabel G., Margaret A. K. Ryan, Tomoko I. Hooper, Tyler C. Smith, Paul J. Amoroso, Edward J. Boyko, Gary D. Gackstetter, Timothy S. Wells, and Nicole S. Bell. "Alcohol Use and Alcohol-Related Problems Before and After Military Combat Deployment." The Journal of the American Medical Association 300, no. 6 (2008): 663–675.

Jenkins, Judy L. "Physiological Effects of Petting a Companion Animal." Psychological Reports 58, no. 1 (1986):21–22.

Koerner, Pete. "Television Is Designed and Intended to Create Anxiety, Stress, and Low Self-Esteem." Ezine Articles. May 28, 2008. http://ezinearticles.com/?Television-Is-Designed-And-Intended-To-Create-Anxiety,-Stress,-And-Low-Self-Esteem&id=1208961.

Ladd, Bronwyn. "How Suicide Rates in the Military Compare to Civilian Populations." Examiner.com. March 24, 2011. http://www.examiner.com/article/how-suicide-rates-the-military-compare-to-civilian-populations.

Leonard, Tom. "US Army in Battle to Cut Divorce Rate." Military Divorce Statistics. January 3, 2005. http://www.divorcereform.org/mil.html.

Levine, Peter A. Waking the Tiger: Healing Trauma. Berkeley, CA: North Atlantic Books, 1997.

Lopes, Paulo. N., Peter Salovey, and Rebecca Straus. "Emotional Intelligence, Personality, and the Perceived Quality of Social Relationships." Personality and Individual Differences 35, no. 3 (2003):641–658.

Lundquist, Jennifer Hicks. "A Comparison of Civilian and Enlisted Divorce Rates during the Early All Volunteer Force Era." Journal of Political and Military Sociology 35, no. 2 (2007):199–217.

Mansfield, Alyssa J., Jay S. Kaufman, Stephen W. Marshall, Bradley N. Gaynes, Joseph P. Morrisey, and Charles C. Engel.

"Deployment and the Use of Mental Health Services among US Army Wives." The New England Journal of Medicine 362, no. 1 (2010):101–109.

Marines.mil. "Never Leave a Marine Behind Annual Suicide Prevention Training and Master Training Team Requirements." Marines.mil. September 20, 2012. http://www.marines.mil/News/Messages/MessagesDisplay/tabid/13286/Article/110342/never-leave-a-Marine-behind-annual-suicide-prevention-training-and-master-train.aspx.

McCraty, Rollin, Mike Atkinson, Dana Tomasino, Jeff Goelitz, and Harvey N. Mayrovitz. "The Impact of an Emotional Self-Management Skills Course on Psychosocial Functioning and Autonomic Recovery to Stress in Middle School Children." Integrative Physiological and Behavioral Science 34, no. 4 (1999):246–268.

Moore, Roland S., Genevieve M. Ames, and Carol B. Cunradi. "Physical and Social Availability of Alcohol for Young Enlisted Naval Personnel In and Around Home Port. Substance Abuse Treatment, Prevention, and Policy 2, no. 17 (2007).

Morrison, Douglas W. How We Heal: Understanding the Mind-Body-Spirit Connection. Berkeley, CA: Mithrandir Trust, 2006.

Nagasawa, Miho, Takefumi Kikusui, Tatsushi Onaka, and Mitsuaki Ohta. "Dog's Gaze at its Owner Increases Owner's Urinary Oxytocin during Social Interaction." Hormones and Behavior 55, no. 3 (2009):434–441.

National Institute on Drug Abuse. "Topics in Brief: Substance Abuse among the Military, Veterans, and their Families." National Institute on Drug Abuse. Last modified April 2011. http://www.drugabuse.gov/publications/topics-in-brief/substance-abuse-among-military-veterans-their-families.

Nova Forgotten Genius. "Plant Medicines." PBS.org. http://www-tc.pbs.org/wgbh/nova/julian/media/lrk-disp-plant-medicines.pdf.

Primack, Brian A., Brandi Swanier, Anna M. Georgiopoulos, Stephanie R. Land, and Michael J. Fine. "Association between Media Use in Adolescence and Depression in Young Adulthood."

Archives of General Psychiatry 66, no. 2 (2009):181–188.

Schneider, Jennifer P. "Compulsive and Addictive Sexual Disorders and the Family." CNS Spectrums 5, no. 10 (2000): 53–62.

Tice, Dianne M., Ellen Bratslavsky, and Roy F. Baumeister. "Emotional Distress Regulation Takes Precedence over Impulse Control: If You Feel Bad, Do It!" Journal of Personality and Social Psychology 80, no. 1 (2001):53–67.

US Department of Defense. "Army Releases December 2012 and Calendar Year 2012 Suicide Information." US Department of Defense. February 1, 2013. http://www.defense.gov/RELEASES/RELEASE.ASPX?RELEASEID=15797.

US Department of Veteran Affairs. "Mental Health Effects of Serving in Afghanistan and Iraq." US Department of Veteran Affairs. Last modified December 20, 2011. http://www.ptsd.va.gov/public/pages/overview-mental-health-effects.asp.

VanFleet, Rise. "Filial Therapy: Strengthening Parent-Child Relationships through Play." PsychINFO (2005): 62-63

Wikipeida. "Slogans of the United States Army." Wikipedia. Last modified May 18, 2013. http://en.wikipedia.org/wiki/Slogans_of_the_United_States_Army.

Wong, Kate. "Study Suggests Emotion Plays a Role in Rational Decision-Making." Scientific American. November 27, 2001. http://www.scientificamerican.com/article.cfm?id=study-suggests-emotion-pl

Wong, Leonard, and Stephen J. Gerras. "The Effects of Multiple Deployments on Army Adolescents." January 2010. http://books.google.com/books?hl=en&lr=&id=fYW192OFPOEC&oi=fnd&pg=PT19&dq=wong+%26+gerras+2010&ots=IKND1de-7Gm&sig=j2qpn_y9ddOXemaFz_x7TN7a50A#.

Zoroya, Gregg. "Female Soldiers' Suicide Rate Triples at War." USA Today. March 18, 2011. http://usatoday30.usatoday.com/news/military/2011-03-18-1Asuicides18_ST_N.htm.

Books and Websites

Books

365 Deployment Days: A Wife's Survival Story by Sara Dawalt

A Family's Guide to the Military for Dummies by Sheryl Garrett and Sue Hoppin

A Year of Absence: Six Women's Stories of Courage by Jessica Redmond

Army Wives by Tanya Biank

Counseling Military Families by Lynn K. Hall

Confessions of a Military Wife by Mollie Gross

Deployment Strategies for Working with Kids in Military Families by Karen Petty

Emotional Intelligence: Why It Can Matter More than IQ by D Goleman

Fighting For your Marriage by Howard Markman, Scott Stanley, and Susan L. Blumberg

For Love and Money: How to Share the Same Checkbook and Still Love Each Other by Bernard E Poduska

God Strong: The Military Wife Spiritual Survival Guide by Sara Horn

Homefront Club by Jacey Eckhart

Hope for the Home Front by Marshele Carter Waddell

Life after Deployment by Karen Pavlicin

Married to the Military: A Survival Guide for Military Wives, Girl-friends, and Women in Uniform by Meredith Leyva

On Combat: The Psychology and Physiology of Deadly Conflict in War and in Peace by Dave Grossman and Loren W. Christensen

On Killing by Lt. Col. Dave Grossman

Separated by Duty, United in Love by Shellie Vandervoorde

Surviving Deployment by Karen M. Pavlicin

The Complete Idiot's Guide to Life as a Military Spouse by Lissa McGrath

The Other Side of War by Zainab Salbi

Til Debt Do Us Part: Balancing Finances, Feelings, and Family by Bernard E. Poduska

Today's Military Wife by Lydia Sloan Cline

While They're at War by Kristin Henderson

Why Does He Do That? Inside the Minds of Angry and Controlling Men by Lundy Bancroft

Internet Sites

Operation: Military Kids: http://www.operationmilitarykids.org

The Military Family Research Institute at Purdue University: http://www.mfri.purdue.edu

Center for the Study of Traumatic Stress: http://centerforthestudy-oftraumaticstress.org/

Military OneSource: http://www.militaryonesource.com

Zero to Three: http://www.zerotothree.org

National Military Family Association: http://www.nmfa.org

About the Author

Dr. Stanley Hall has worked with service members in the US Navy and Marine Corps since 2009 working in the Deployment Health Clinic using the best training available to help families work through the symptoms associated with PTSD and TBI. Dr. Hall has also worked extensively with couples who are struggling in abusive relationships on the marine base. Dr. Hall has years of experience using Heart Math (an extensively researched treatment) to help individuals and families address issues of anger, depression, anxiety, and stress. Dr. Hall also has been practicing Eye Movement Desensitization and Reprocessing (EMDR) and Prolonged Exposure (PE) to help hundreds of individuals work through traumatic memories from childhood abuse and combat.

About the Publisher

Welcome to a place where mothers are celebrated, not compared. Where heart is at the center of our families, and family at the center of our homes. Where boo boos are still kissed, cake beaters are still licked, and mistakes are still okay. Welcome to a place where books—and family—are beautiful. Familius: a book publisher dedicated to helping families be happy.

Familius was founded in 2012 with the intent to align the founders' love of publishing and family with the digital publishing renaissance which occurred simultaneously with the Great Recession. The founders believe that the traditional family is the basic unit of society, and that a society is only as strong as the families that create it. Familius's mission is to help families be happy. We invite you to participate with us in strengthening your family by being part of the Familius family. Go to www.familius.com to subscribe and receive information about our books, articles, and videos.

Website: www.familius.com
Facebook: www.facebook.com/paterfamilius
Twitter: @familiustalk, @paterfamilius1
Pinterest: www.pinterest.com/familius